Fan Letters to a Stripper

A Patti Waggin Tale

Bob Brill

Schiffer Publishing Ltd
4880 Lower Valley Road Atglen, Pennsylvania 19310

Dedication

My wife Claudia has put up with so many of my projects over the years and continues to be the person who says one of her goals in life is to keep my ego in check. Without her help and support, as well as her encouragement to do what I know I can do, this project would never have gotten off the ground.

To my children Bobby, Julia, and James, I continue to hear the call of "research Dad, research" as well as "go for it." They all pointed out while looking through the letters and photographs to place in this first book, "this is something I never thought I would ever do with my father."

To my mom, Florence, who won't understand why her son wrote a book about a stripper; to my father, Jim, who would give me *that* glance and who encouraged me that I could do whatever I wanted to do in this world, I say thank you for your love and support.

No such dedication would be complete without a few others being named: my sister, June, who planned a surprise birthday party and schemed to get me out of the house so I could buy my first pack of baseball cards with a Don Rudolph card in it and my brother, Jim, who is laughing even as we speak about me writing about a stripper. Also my partners in this project, who just happen to be lawyers, Amy and Terry, who believed in me enough to agree to come on board as partners.

And, of course, to the Good Lord above who gave me the passion for a project I've waited my entire life to put between two hardbound covers.

Acknowledgments

I wish to thank my research assistant Lisa Joe, who spent days upon days searching and sorting; Sy Berger, who gave the go ahead to the back of Don Rudolph's 1959 Topps card, which had a cartoon of Patti Waggin dancing on a table; and Julena, Robert, Charles, Don, and Patti – all of whom contributed in some small way, and in some cases obviously larger ways, to making this book possible.

Other Schiffer Books on Related Subjects
The Bare Truth: Stars of Burlesque from the '40s and '50s. Len Rothe. ISBN: 0764306030. $19.95
The Queens of Burlesque: Vintage Photographs from the 1940s and 1950s. Len Rothe. ISBN: 0764304496. $19.95
Striptease Artists of the 1950s. Bunny Yeager. ISBN: 9780764328008. $24.95

Library of Congress Control Number: 2009927266

Covers and book designed by Bruce Waters
Type set in Zaph Chancery Bd BT/News Gothic BT

ISBN: 978-0-7643-3329-3
Printed in China

Schiffer Books are available at special discounts for bulk purchases for sales promotions or premiums. Special editions, including personalized covers, corporate imprints, and excerpts can be created in large quantities for special needs. For more information contact the publisher:

Published by Schiffer Publishing Ltd.
4880 Lower Valley Road
Atglen, PA 19310
Phone: (610) 593-1777; Fax: (610) 593-2002
E-mail: Info@schifferbooks.com

For the largest selection of fine reference books on this and related subjects, please visit our web site at **www.schifferbooks.com**
We are always looking for people to write books on new and related subjects. If you have an idea for a book please contact us at the above address.

This book may be purchased from the publisher.
Include $5.00 for shipping.
Please try your bookstore first.
You may write for a free catalog.

Contents

Foreword

On June 26, 1959, "little Robert" Brill, as they called him, purchased his first pack of Topps trading cards. It was his sixth birthday. As he perused through the pack, he found something odd. The back of each card had a cartoon, which described something interesting about the player. On the back of Don Rudolph's card, the cartoon was not about the Chicago White Sox pitcher but about his wife.

There, underneath a sketch of a woman dancing on a table with a ballplayer sitting at the table looking up her skirt, read the caption "Don's wife is a professional dancer."

Even a six year old kid, pre-hormones raging, knew this was odd. It stuck in his mind and over the years he attempted bits of research with few results. That is until the Internet. Robert, now known as Bob Brill with over thirty years background in radio and broadcast journalism, also wrote a sports column. It was time to write the story.

As it turns out, not only was he amazed at what he learned, but he had come to find out Patti Waggin (now easily recognized as the woman in the cartoon on the card) and Don Rudolph lived within a mile or so of where Robert grew up. The couple banked at the institution across the street from Robert's house where he had his first bank account at the same time.

He would later learn Don coached Colt League Baseball in the same league, coaching against some of the same kids Robert would play with and know in school. This was all too bizarre to imagine back in 1959. It fueled a passion to turn this story into more. We hope you enjoy *Fan Letters to a Stripper* because we have two follow up books planned looking into different areas of Patti's life and career, which we hope you will find fascinating as well as touching. We are also planning a feature film.

Fan Letters is a real work of love. I wanted to show how a stripper, or exotic dancer, is also a working, living, breathing human being with a family life outside the stage persona. I also wanted to show the impact fans can have on a performer and why such letters are important. Further, I wish to explore and better understand the human mind, which motivates some to heap adoration upon someone they don't even know.

Although in the days Patti was performing, meeting was easier than it is today and will ever be again. The fan merely had to go to the show and pay his 50-cents and be there. A backstage meeting could be requested for a photo opportunity and if granted what else could they ask for?

The "what else" is in the letters in the pages you are about to read. I have found the story of Patti and Don a fabulous tale of two professionals, deeply in love, from drastically different backgrounds, to be an unbelievably good story. To quote Ray Kinsella, "A long story but a really good story."

Who Is Patti Waggin and Why Should I Care?

Born Patricia Hardwick in humble surroundings in northern California in 1926, Patti was raised by her mother. She had several half brothers, each with a different father. Her own father was a bit of a mystery to Patti. At one point, later in life, her mother confided to her that Patti's dad was either an Italian stagehand or a dancer she had met back in her own performing days. Driven to rise above her modest upbringing, in the 1940s and 1950s Patti took the burlesque stage by storm. With her good looks and athleticism, Patti quickly made a name ... several names actually ... for herself. She was The Educated Torso, The Sex Oomph Girl, the Fresh-faced Girl Next Door, and ... most memorably ... Patti Waggin. However, Patti was loved most by her peers and her admirers for her generous spirit. Patti was considered to be the friendliest of all the burlesque headliners, the one who diligently answered all her fan mail.

But we are getting ahead of ourselves. Patti's early life gives us glimpses of the public persona's true nature and private passions. From an early age, the future Patti Waggin developed a love for motorcycles. She was equally at home riding, or racing, Indians or Harleys.

Prior to taking to the burlesque stage, Patti tried her hand at theater at Chico State College. She also showed her competitive edge, an edge that served her well in burlesque, as she competed in team sports such as basketball and baseball and individually against men on motorcycles.

In her early years, Patti's name changed twice. At sixteen, she married Doug Craig, her first love. By college, Doug was no longer in the picture and Patti married local motorcycle icon Bill Brownell. Between marriages there would be a number of love affairs. While Bill Brownell, Chico, California's Indian distributor, could not hold onto Patti, Patti held on to the Brownell name during the 1940s, in her early years on the stage.

In 1950, Patti changed her look, dropping the sex kitten facade that had worked for her in her teens. She replaced the child-like kitty with a more grown up, sultry look, including a new hairdo with bangs. Patti's new persona caused a stir; she closely resembled Bettie Page. People wondered who was copying whom? Today, Bettie Page's website declares she adopted her look in 1947. Others are not so sure.

No matter, in January 1955 Bettie Page made a splash when she appeared in an early issue of the fledgling Playboy magazine. By October, Patti had followed, featured in an article entitled, "The Stripper Goes to College." It seems an enterprising young man running for student body president at Southern Cal struck on a novel get out the vote approach, hiring Patti to perform her sultry dance at a party. Southern Cal's president banned Patti from campus, but the show went on and the article followed.

In a humorous aside, one of the fan letters that follow is from a fellow who sent Patti an early photo of what he imagined to be her. Patti made a note on that letter to kindly thank the gentleman for the picture of Bettie Page.

In the midst of the heady years of her career in the 1950s, Patti met Don Rudolph, a tall, lanky left-handed pitcher playing minor league baseball in the Chicago White Sox farm system. Rudolph met Patti in Colorado Springs and pursued her diligently. For a time, she denied him; then she fell for him. They married in the mid-1950s. Initially, for the sakes of both their careers, the marriage was kept secret. Both felt their fans just would not understand, to say nothing of the White Sox management. In time, however, the news came out and the world moved on. As will be seen from the letters, Patti's fans promptly became Don's fans, keeping track of his career as the years went by. Head over heels for each other, when Patti and Don wrote to each other while Don was away, they used pet names to show their affection; his was "Daddy Donnie" and hers was "Stinky." Stinky?

Given her competitive nature, Patti was a determined self-promoter. When Don married Patti, he jumped into the promotion game with both feet, advancing Patti's career at every opportunity. As her new manager, Don adjusted her performance schedule and locations around his minor league travel schedule so that they could be together whenever possible.

Together Patti and Don had one child, a daughter named Julena. Sadly, the love of Patti's life was taken from her all too soon. Don died in a trucking accident in 1968.

Patti was devastated. She suffered with bouts of depression, but her daughter, a number of boyfriends, her dogs, bowling nights with friends she and Don had made together, and wild rides on her Harley Davidson all helped her through. Patti's later years found her content with life. She passed away in 1992. Her daughter states, however, that none of her fellow luminaries of the burlesque stage attended the funeral.

Now that we have a brief history of Patti's life and career, let's take a look at how the fans saw Patti. Fans wrote frequently and with enthusiasm because Patti understood what they needed from her in return. Her correspondence saw them through all their trials and tribulations at home and at war. Patti's fans felt she was more than a corresponding celebrity; they considered her a friend and confidante.

These letters also provide a revealing portrait of Patti's fans themselves. Some of the letters are insightful, funny, and very nice, while others are unsettling. Exploring these pages, you will meet average fans seeking a few publicity photos, a young solider in North Korea in 1952 seeking pin-up photos for himself and the guys, and a few characters who wanted to take Patti away from it all. There is also a touching letter from a grieving daughter writing on behalf of her father, who was a big fan and had recently died. She thanked Patti for being her father's friend.

There is a glimpse of a different time and sensibility in this correspondence. Patti received the bulk of her fan mail, especially in her later years, at home. Twice over the years her home address was the headquarters for her fan club. Today we shudder at the thought of being so easily accessible to total strangers and imagine all sorts of dire outcomes.

The letters are presented here as they were written. I have not changed a thing. Some had to be retyped solely for clarity. Accompanying these letters are professional and candid photos of Patti, her family, friends, and fans. Through all of these sources, you will soon discover not only the life of a stripper, but also the life and times of a wonderful, loving, and much loved human being.

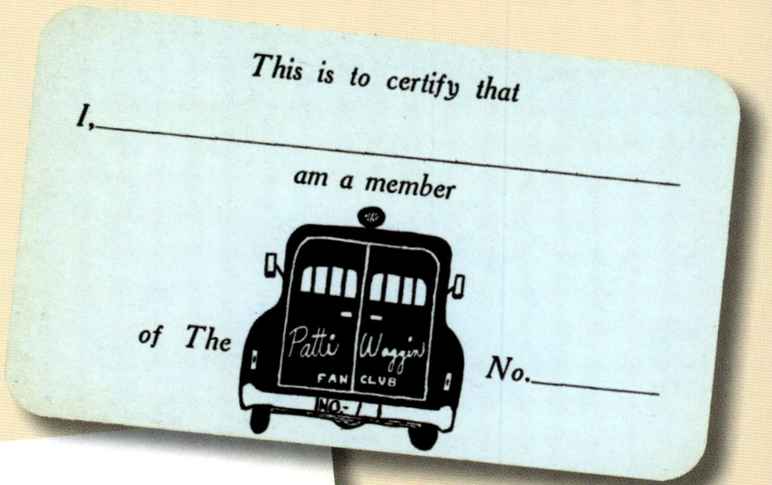

This is to certify that

I, ____________________

am a member

of The Patti Waggin' FAN CLUB *No.* ________

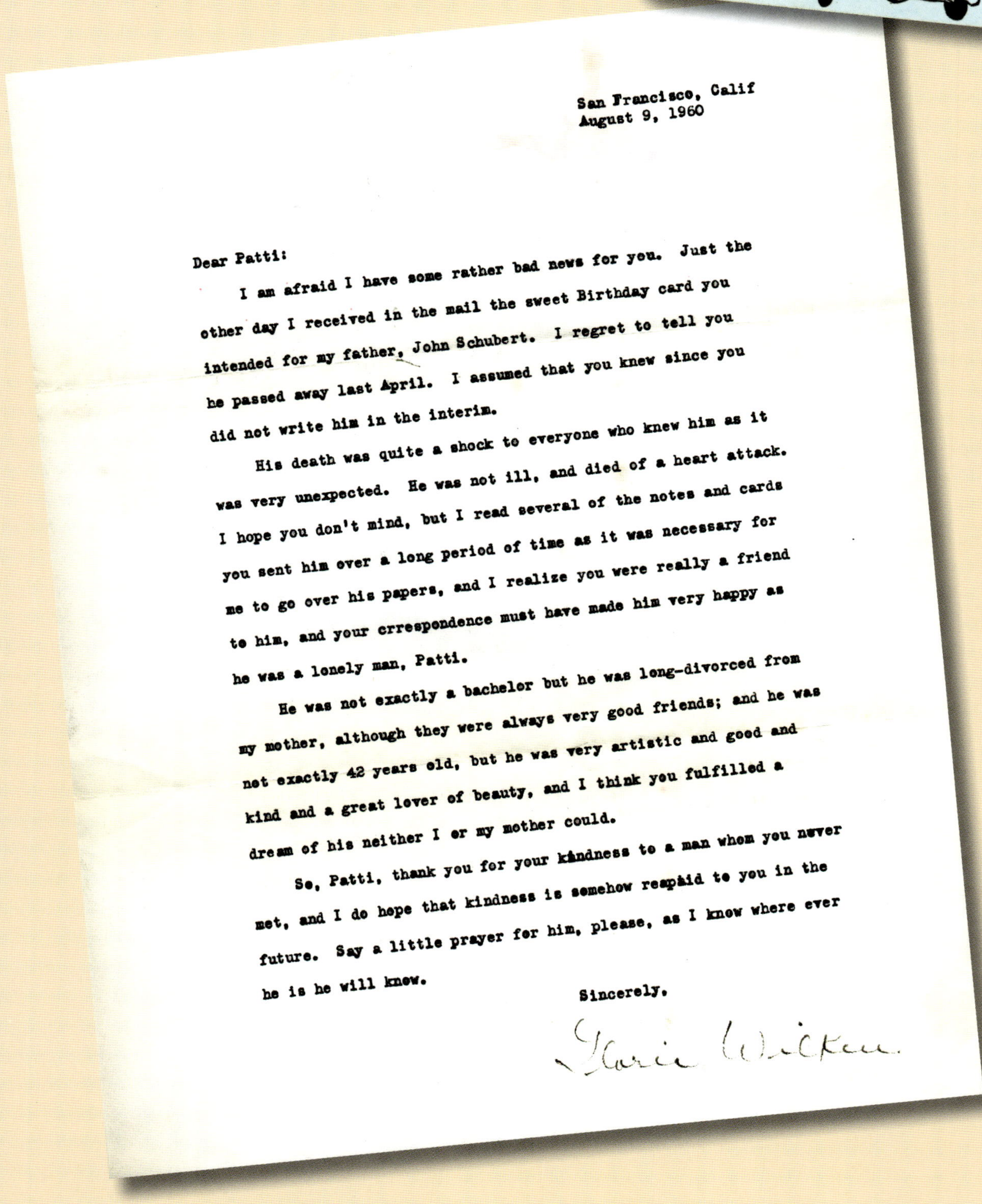

San Francisco, Calif
August 9, 1960

Dear Patti:

I am afraid I have some rather bad news for you. Just the
other day I received in the mail the sweet Birthday card you
intended for my father, John Schubert. I regret to tell you
he passed away last April. I assumed that you knew since you
did not write him in the interim.

His death was quite a shock to everyone who knew him as it
was very unexpected. He was not ill, and died of a heart attack.
I hope you don't mind, but I read several of the notes and cards
you sent him over a long period of time as it was necessary for
me to go over his papers, and I realize you were really a friend
to him, and your crrespondence must have made him very happy as
he was a lonely man, Patti.

He was not exactly a bachelor but he was long-divorced from
my mother, although they were always very good friends; and he was
not exactly 42 years old, but he was very artistic and good and
kind and a great lover of beauty, and I think you fulfilled a
dream of his neither I or my mother could.

So, Patti, thank you for your kindness to a man whom you never
met, and I do hope that kindness is somehow respaid to you in the
future. Say a little prayer for him, please, as I know where ever
he is he will know.

Sincerely,

Keith
Bernard

Barstow Aug 3, 1953.
P. O. Box - 722.

Dear Miss Brownell:

Having noticed your picture in the Mirror, I was rather surprised that it wasn't of the cheesecake type. The picture is a rather lovely one, and the thought struck me that perhaps you would part with a photograph of this very picture.

Perhaps if you are unable to send one of this type, will you be kind enough to return this one to me, as I have a nice place at the top of my mirror, here in my trailer for the picture.

Thanking you very much for your thoughtfulness, I remain one of your admiring public.

Sincerely
R. W. Holston
Richard W. Holston

August 7, 1960

Dear Lovely Darling Patti,

I was so happy and pleased to receive a letter from you and the photograph of your lovliness so sweetly autographed with love.

I take the Vista bus every morning in front of the Burbank Theatre at 6th & main streets in L.A. at 4:55 a.m. When I saw the large picture of you on display in front of the theatre on the right side in your bra and small girdle I said to myself there is the lovliest and most beautiful woman I have ever seen. In this picture I see the highest degree of femininity in all it's perfection personalized by you. And you have such a sweet spiritual face also. It is so sweet of you to share such unique beauty with the public. God bless you for it.

I am enclosing a check for a copy of this pose. Please autograph it with love to Joe.

I said to myself I am going to have a wife just like Patti in all her lovliness. Then I thought why not Patti herself. After all the best is none too good for the Irish. Why not? I have been alone three years. I have a world of sweet tender love and respect to give the woman who will share my life.

I went to church to day with my father. I am enclosing a program. Dearest Patti may I see you when you come to L.A. again.

With all my love as long as I live I remain your most ardent admirer and loving you every minute of every day.

Joseph G. Morrow, Senior
5653 ½ Stoll Drive
Highland Park Los Angeles 42, Calif.

The Atchison, Topeka and Santa Fe Railway Company

COAST LINES

FREIGHT DEPOT—970 East Third Street

L. J. RAY,
Freight Agent
JOHN J. MORGAN,
Assistant Agent
F. M. WILLIAMS,
Assistant Agent

Telephone:
Mutual 0111 x581

Mail Address:
P. O. Box 3276
Terminal Annex

Los Angeles 54, Calif.

In Reply Refer to July 5 1953

To Patti :

The girl who stole "Thunder's" thunder. In addition to being a better dancer , you are much more appealing in your little sailor suit than "Thunder" in her "standard acouterments" Despite the fact that it's true , it may sound like a left handed compliment to say that I think you were without a doubt the pretiest one in the whole show. (the "show" being last night). And speaking of the "show" , I'm curious to know just what it was that got you so curious just as the curtain went down about 11:30. You looked like you either saw a familiar face or something very unusual.

Not that I expect you to take leave of your good sense and say "yes" to anything I might ask, but that's no reason not to ask. One of the many things that I am not - is what is referred to as a " stage door johnny" or a"Wolf" in the full sense of the word. Two things that "Johnny" has that I don't,is a big new car and a big roll. I'M just a character who drives a 41 De Soto and works for the Atchison Topeka and Santa Fe from 3pm to 11pm - officially a "Car Clerk" , which is what I am doing right now (4pm Sunday) and will be doing for the next two and a half weeks before I return to " California" which to me means the " Bay Area".

A pessimist - so they tell me - is one who says "The cup is half empty" while an optomist says " the cup is half full" - MY cup is half full just from having seen you at a distance - it could be FULL if I could spend a simple evening with you just doing nothing but being platonic - or as platonic as you want it. My idea of a simple evening - since I'm no great gun at doing anything but spotting beauty - consists of dinner a show and a night cap. Interested ? or do you still have all of your senses? If you're even only partially interested in a "simple" evening but can't quite say "yes" you could call me and we could talk. ?????????

Optomistically

Ben

SANTA FE—DEDICATED TO SERVICE

Patti's favorite dance partner never fussed and always took direction.

Wed-17-52

Dear Miss Patti,

Just got a chance to look at your act. I thought you were very versatile and quite lovely. I still can't understand why one like you so, charming and there seems to be so much talent, why it is wasted on "burlesque." Well that comes under the heading of none of my business. I don't mean to criticize and I am not. But that recalls something that happened a while ago. I was told by a friend, "by the way this friend went to church," anyway he told me that there was a girl singing in the meeting. And she had a voice out of this world. So here I go to see and hear this. Well I never heard anything like it. So I told my boss – Mr. De Miller. And he came down for a hear too? Well he offers the girl everything but she said that god gave her the voice and she was going to use it in his work. And also that she was very happy just the way things were. But my god where that girl could have gone with that voice. But after seeing you, I just had to drop you a line to tell you I did so much enjoy your act and I wish I had a 8 x 10 picture autographed to me. And the next time those mugs want a good dancer I'll come up with a picture of a real good one. I do wish you would let me know who your agent is. Just in case. So if you will send me a picture of two. I sure would appreciate it and I do think you are tops. So Miss Patti just lots of good luck and success with a little bit of happiness along the line always.

Thank you for reading.

Very Truly Yours,

Carey
CH Smith
738 Union Ave L.A.

Pi Kappa Phi
Maker of Woman

Tues. Aug 25, 1959

Patti...

Wow!! Recived your letter and foto's and thats all I can say, Wow!! Looking forward to additional pictures of the *most* in beauty. I enjoyed your fan club card very much and will carry it always. A I would like very much to have a booking list of your coming appearances if it is possibly. If I know the fellows at the frat. they will want a giant photo for the fireplace. Will let you know as soon as I get back to school. Best of Luck to the Best in the League Love

Your greatest Admirer
R. N. Gooldy

(P.S. over)

Dear Don & Patti,

Just a few lines to let you know that your Pittsburgh Contingent of your fan clubs sill think of you – haven't heard of you people for a while so I'm wondering what's been happening with you. My little nephew still walks around dressed like a Cincinatti Red. I painted his batting helmet for him Red & White with a Red "C" on it. He's been looking for Don's name in all the sports news etc & so have I for a matter of fact. What are you up to Don??? Also Patti It seems as though you have both disappeared form the scene.

I was with Larry Elgart for about 9 mos. But I quit recently. We made a fw albums for victor while I was on the band abut they didn't do too well as far as I know. At present I'm trying to get my unemployment checks from N.Y. State if I can. I intend to go to L.A. for a while as I have a chance for some jobs out there with my Uncle.

So please if you get a chance drop a line and let me know where you both are & what you're doing. As I say I haven't seen anything about you two in the various trade papers.

I recently got your x-mas card and I thought it was nice. So at the risk of being repetitious Please drop a line on occasion and keep in touch.

Your friend
Frank La Marca
105 Crawford Ave.
Pgh 2, Penna

P.P.S. I've written a few original tunes you may be interested in if you think you may be of any use to you let me know and you can have them.

P.P.S. My nephew dropped you a line. He meant to ask for a ball if it's not too much trouble.

NAVY SUPPLY STORE
Lee
ION ALLS & OVERALLS
546
& NAVY SUPPLY STORE 546
546 SPORT
BURBANK
ON STAGE IN PERSON
PATTI WAGGIN
THE SEX-OOMPH DOLL
NEW SHOW FRIDAY
GIRLS BEAUTIFUL GIRLS
PACIFIC LOAN CO.
MONEY TO LOAN
PACIFIC LOAN CO.
STATE
DIAMONDS
WE LOAN
Largest

DEAR VALENTINE...
You're the SALT of the EARTH.........

And I Kinda like the SHAKER it comes in, too!
The "Waggin Club"
Kenneth Helton
Kent Pierce
Ralph Gemmer
Tom Grieman

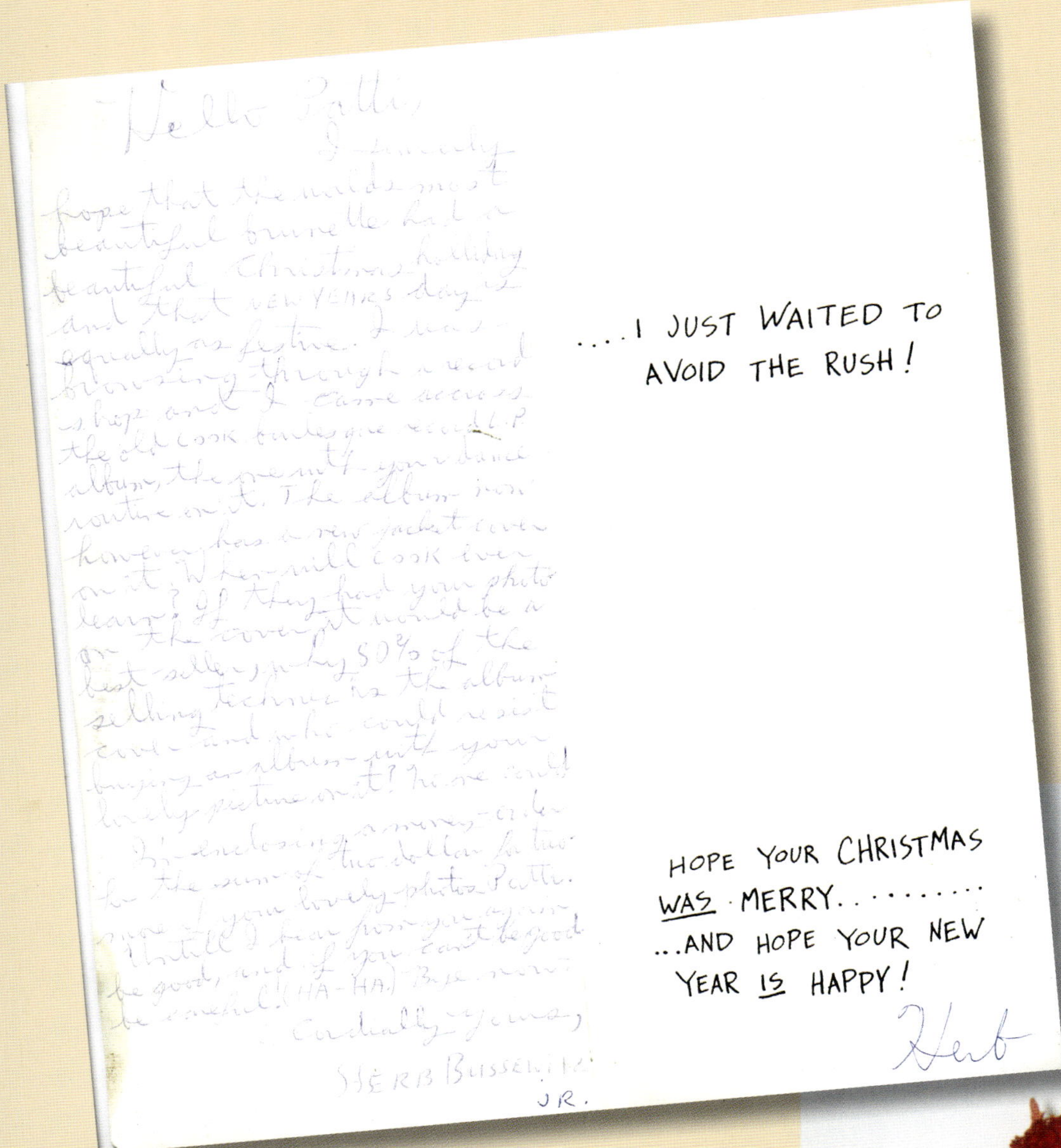

Hello Patti,

I sincerely hope that the world's most beautiful brunette had a beautiful Christmas holiday and that New Year's day is equally as festive. I was browsing through a record shop and I came across the old cook burlesque record L.P. album, the one with your dance routine on it. The album now however has a new jacket cover on it. When will cook ever learn? If they had your photo on the cover it would be a best seller, [illegible] 80% of the selling [illegible] is the album cover — and who could resist buying an album with your lovely picture on it! [illegible]

I'm enclosing a money-order for the sum of two dollars for two more of your lovely photos Patti. Untill I hear from you again be good, and if you can't be good be careful! (HA-HA) Bye now.

Cordially yours,

Herb Bussewitz Jr.

....I JUST WAITED TO AVOID THE RUSH!

HOPE YOUR CHRISTMAS WAS MERRY.........
...AND HOPE YOUR NEW YEAR IS HAPPY!

Herb

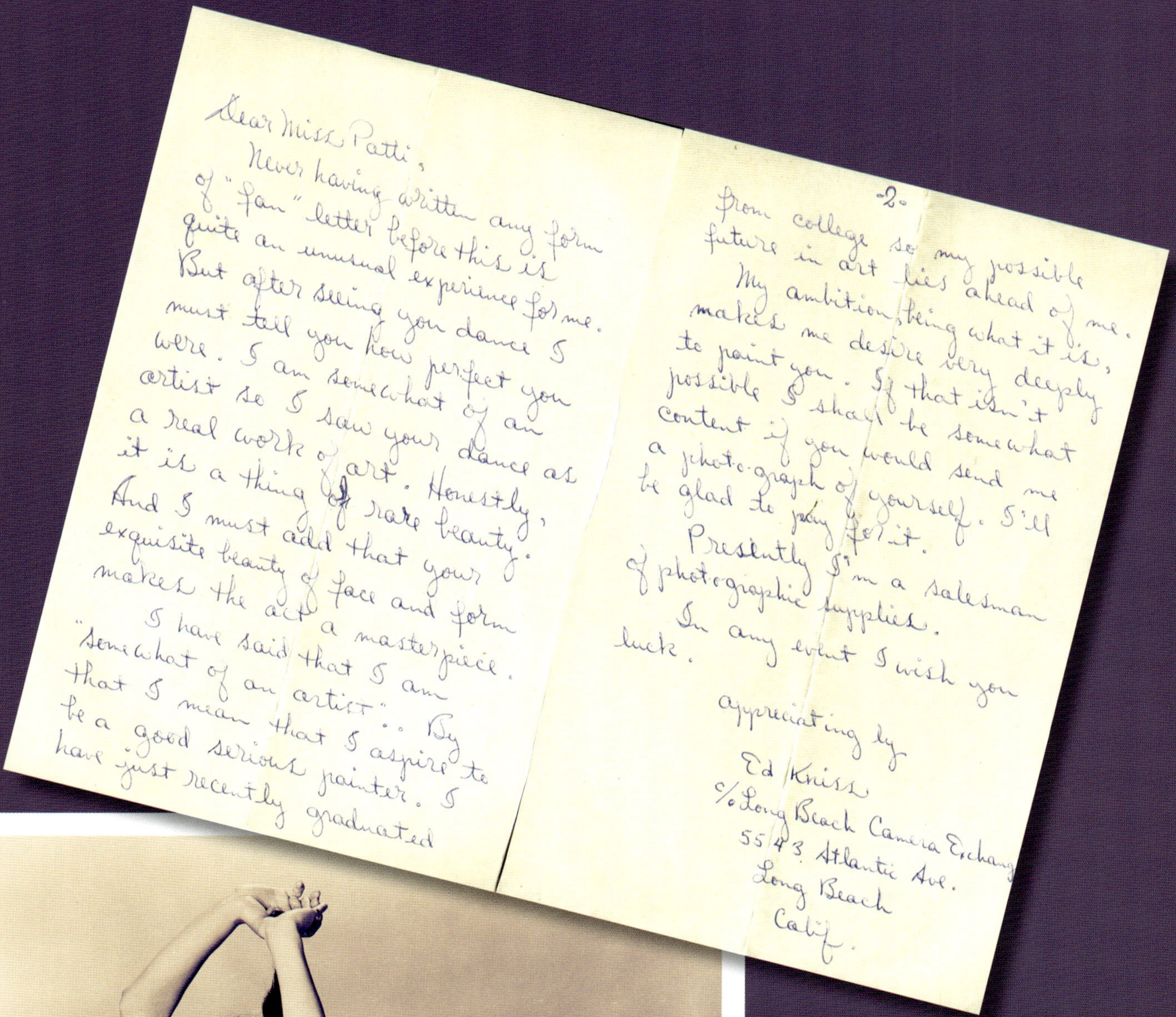

Dear Miss Patti,

Never having written any form of "fan" letter before this is quite an unusual experience for me. But after seeing you dance I must tell you how perfect you were. I am somewhat of an artist so I saw your dance as a real work of art. Honestly, it is a thing of rare beauty. And I must add that your exquisite beauty of face and form makes the act a masterpiece.

I have said that I am "somewhat of an artist".. By that I mean that I aspire to be a good serious painter. I have just recently graduated

-2-

from college so my possible future in art lies ahead of me.

My ambition, being what it is, makes me desire very deeply to paint you. If that isn't possible I shall be somewhat content if you would send me a photo-graph of yourself. I'll be glad to pay for it.

Presently I'm a salesman of photographic supplies.

In any event I wish you luck.

appreciatingly

Ed Kriss
c/o Long Beach Camera Exchang
5543 Atlantic Ave.
Long Beach
Calif.

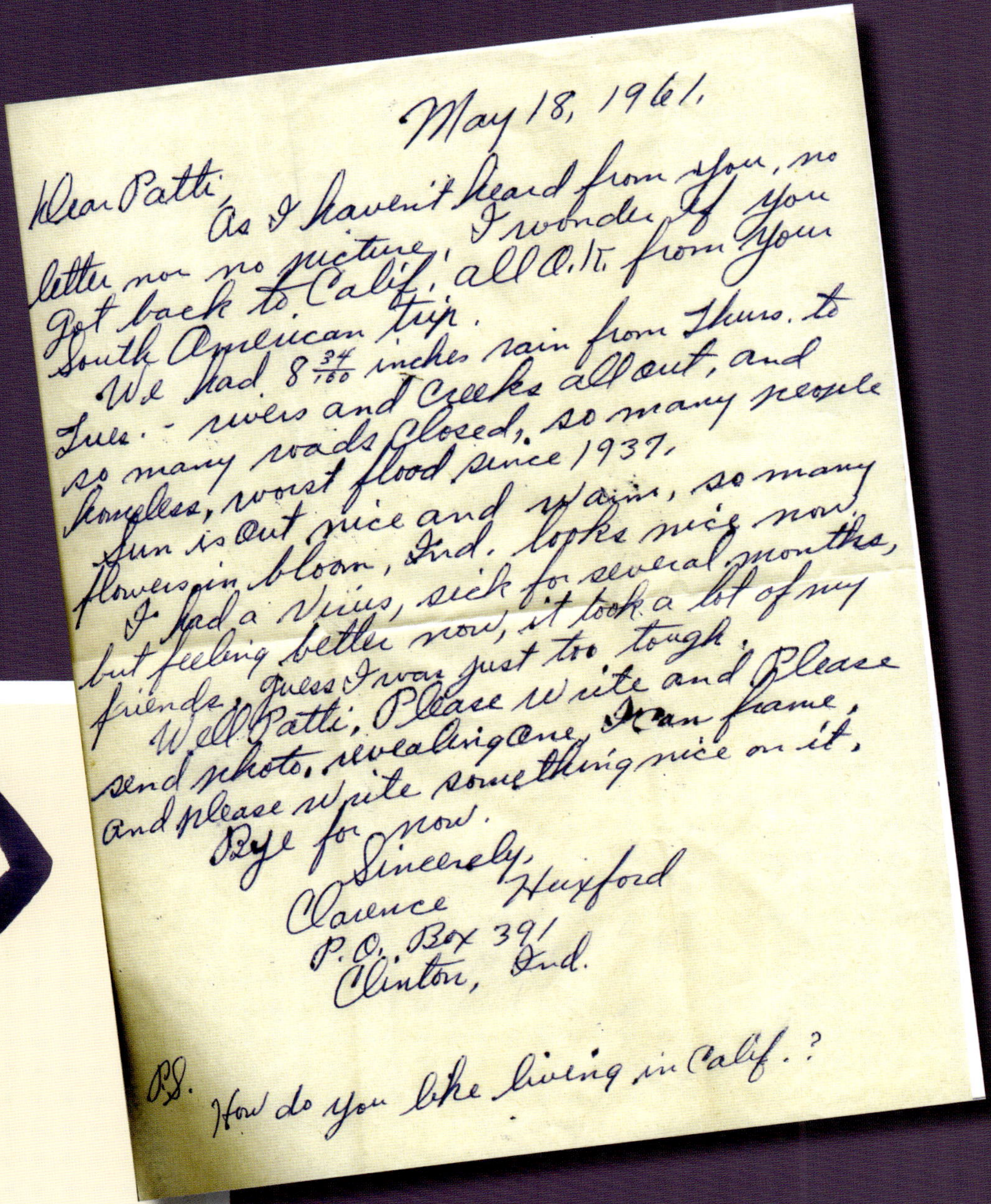

May 18, 1961.

Dear Patti,

As I haven't heard from you, no letter nor no picture, I wonder if you got back to Calif. all O.K. from your South American trip.

We had $8\frac{34}{100}$ inches rain from Thurs. to Tues. - rivers and creeks all out, and so many roads closed, so many people homeless, worst flood since 1937.

Sun is out nice and warm, so many flowers in bloom, Ind. looks nice now.

I had a virus, sick for several months, but feeling better now, it took a lot of my friends, guess I was just too tough.

Well Patti, Please write and Please send photo, revealing one, I can frame, and please write something nice on it.

Bye for now.

Sincerely,
Clarence Huxford
P.O. Box 391
Clinton, Ind.

P.S. How do you like living in Calif.?

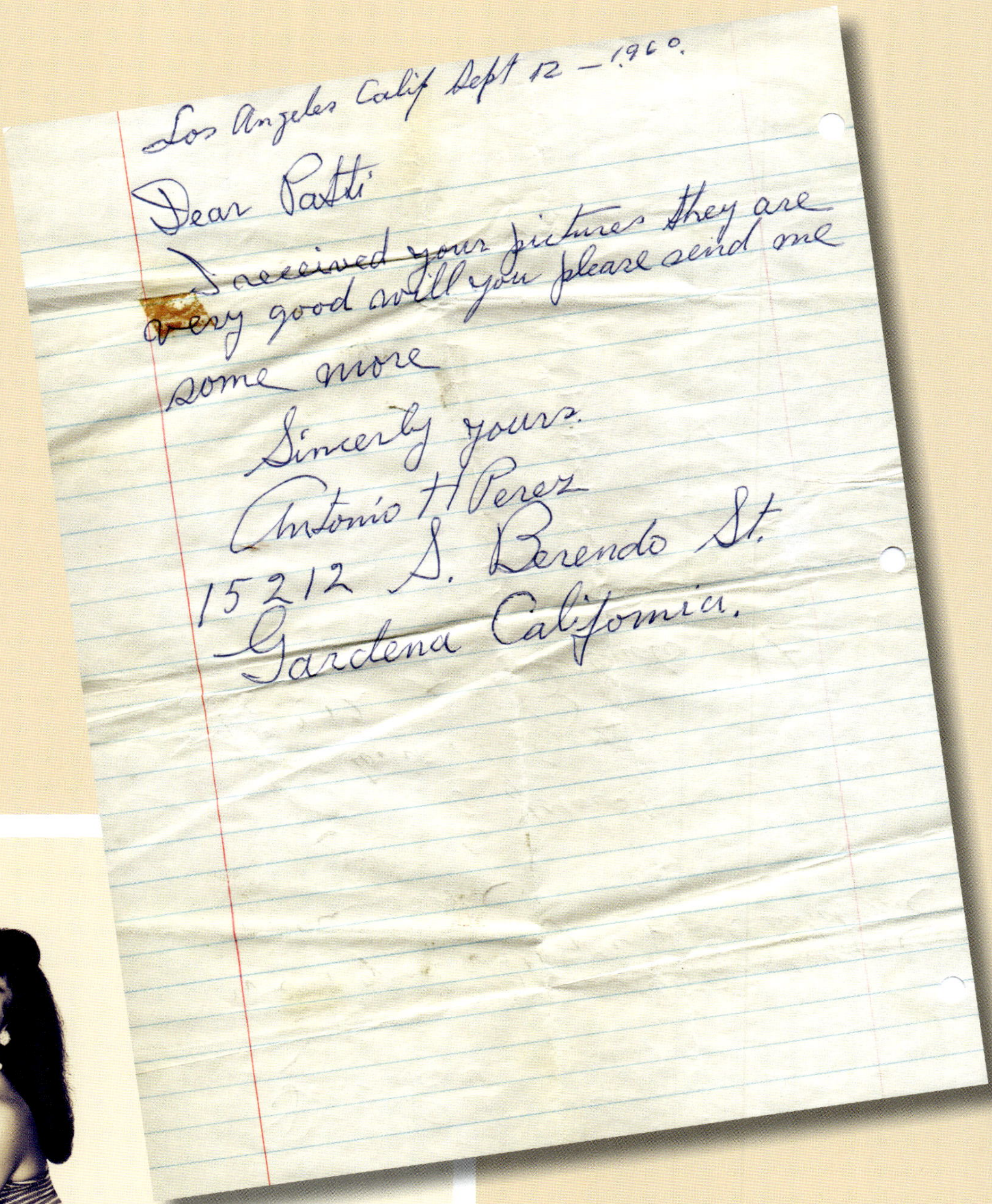
Los Angeles Calif Sept 12 – 1960.

Dear Patti

I received your pictures they are very good will you please send me some more

Sincerly yours.

Antonio H Perez

15212 S. Berendo St.

Gardena California.

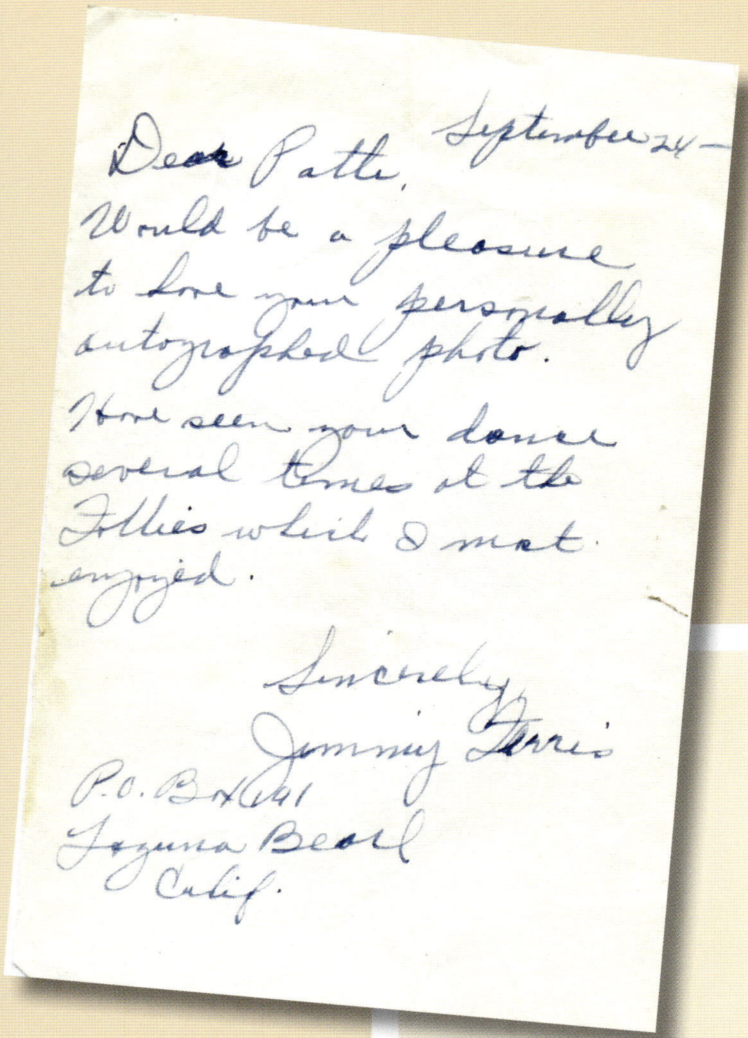
September 24 —

Dear Patti,

Would be a pleasure to have your personally autographed photo.

Have seen your dance several times at the Follies which I most enjoyed.

Sincerely,

Jimmy Ferris

P.O. Box 41

Laguna Beach

Calif.

September 8, 1960

Dear Patti',

Just a short note to let you know I have changed my address as follows:

Old address: 60 So. ROOSEVELT AVE. APT. 4 PASADENA

New address: ROGER L. WILSON 3053 LA CORONA AVE. ALTADENA, CALIF.

Also, please send me ~~no~~ more pictures. Enclosed find one dollar for charges. The first picture was great, but how about seeing a little more of you? Thanks again.

Best wishes,

Roger Wilson

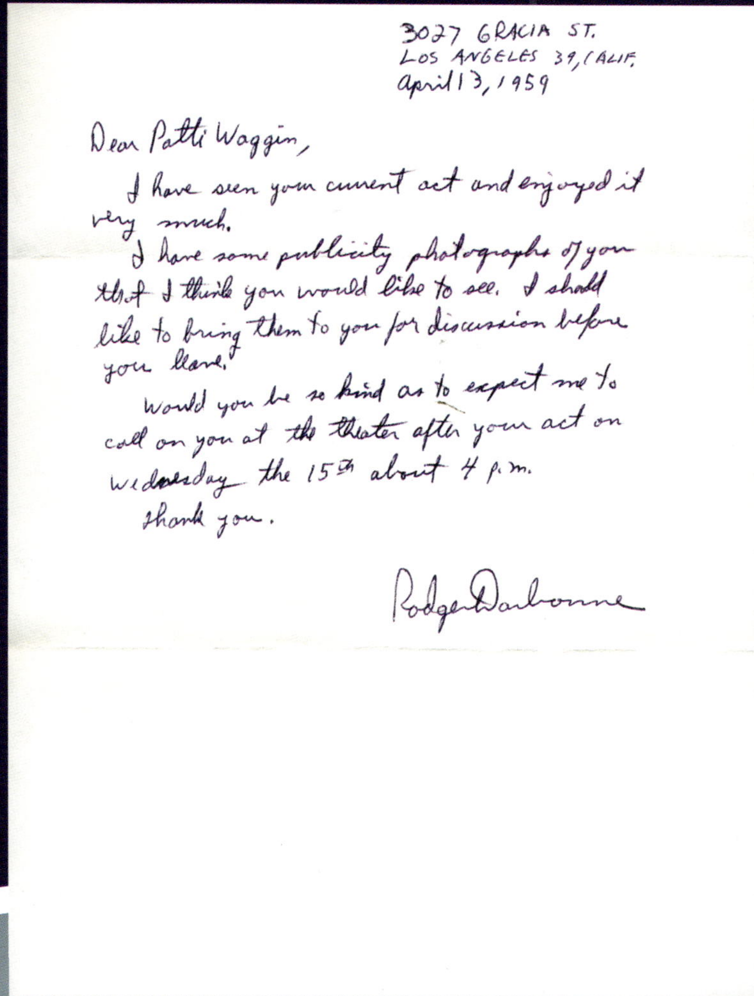

3027 GRACIA ST.
LOS ANGELES 39, CALIF.
April 13, 1959

Dear Patti Waggin,

I have seen your current act and enjoyed it very much.

I have some publicity photographs of you that I think you would like to see. I should like to bring them to you for discussion before you leave.

Would you be so kind as to expect me to call on you at the theater after your act on Wednesday the 15th about 4 p.m.

Thank you.

Rodger Darbonne

Hi Patti,

I bet your surpsied to hear from me again. I've been meaning to write before this but I've been tied down with studying.

I'm going to school fulltime at Prince Georges College and man it sure isn't like high school. You've really got to apply yourself. I'm trying.

My course is a general one now. My clsses are: Fundamentals of Speech, Composition and Contemporary Literature, General Psychology and Mathematics for Liberart Arts. These are all pretty tough.

I hope you're allright and everyone else.

Tell Don that Mike Epstein, the Senators 1st baseman, goes to school here too. I sure hope Boston wins the Series.

Oh, that girl, Laurie and I broke up or I should say quit dating.

Patti, that hurt when you asked me if I was getting married in your last letter. Randy's back from California now. He's now going to Maryland University and Jimmy is back at Frostburg. I am playing football for the school. We had our first game today. We lost.

I hope you know that I don't want you to forget me. I could never forget you, Patti.

I shaved my beard off before school started. It was really looking nice. But my parents thought I looked like a bum. I'm still the same guy as I was.

How was your trip to Oregon? I sure hope it was a nice one. My buddy Dave and I go down to Virginia sometimes on weekends and camp out. We are planning on going back down again on the 19th of October. We have off those days.

I don't know why but when I go down there I find I <u>really</u> miss you. I hope I still mean something to you. That's really all I care about.

Please, Patti, write to me.

Ralph

PATTI WAGGIN
Patti Waggin
FAN CLUB
NO. 1
Patti Waggin
Patti Waggin
"the co-ed with the educated torso"
Patti Waggin

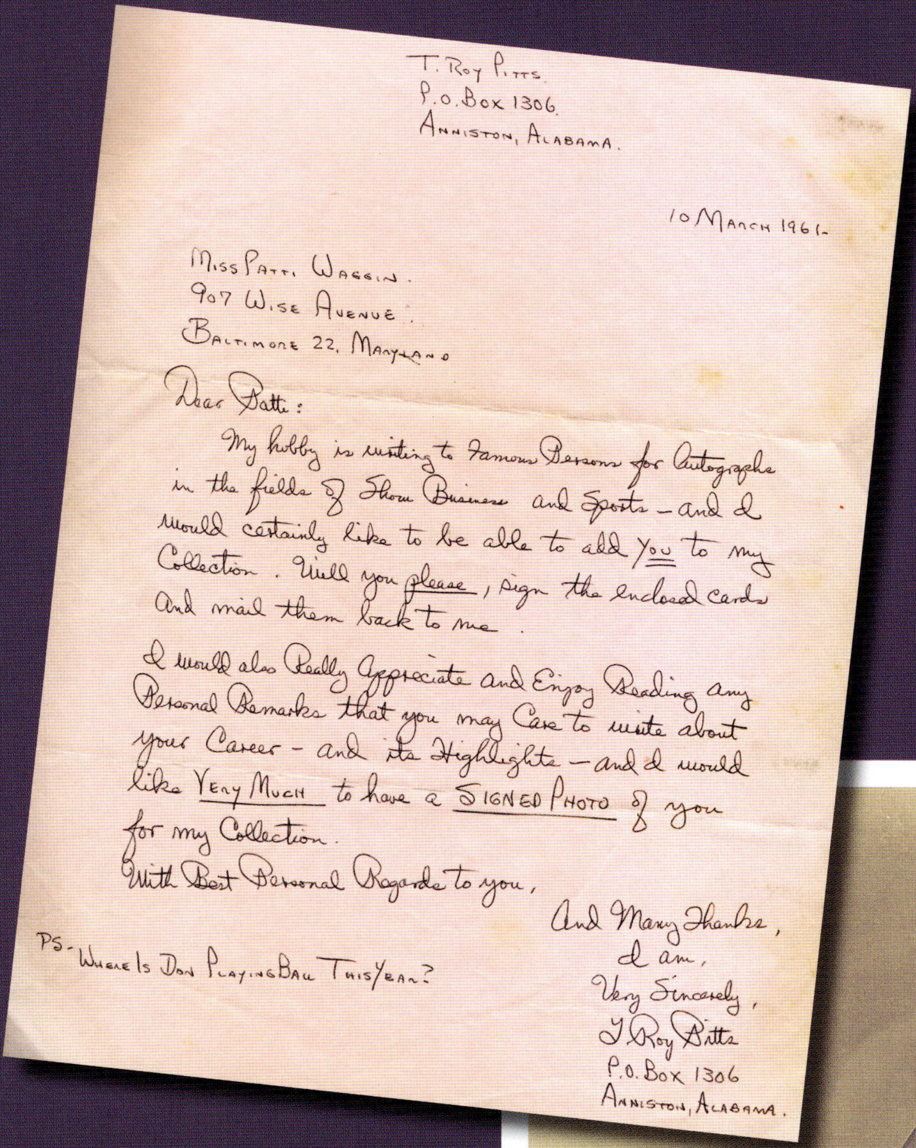

T. Roy Pitts
P.O. Box 1306.
Anniston, Alabama.

10 March 1961.

Miss Patti Waggin.
907 Wise Avenue.
Baltimore 22, Maryland

Dear Patti:

My hobby is writing to Famous Persons for Autographs in the fields of Show Business and Sports – and I would certainly like to be able to add You to my Collection. Will you please, sign the enclosed cards and mail them back to me.

I would also Really Appreciate and Enjoy Reading any Personal Remarks that you may Care to write about your Career – and its Highlights – and I would like Very Much to have a Signed Photo of you for my Collection.

With Best Personal Regards to you,

And Many Thanks,
I am,
Very Sincerely,
T. Roy Pitts
P.O. Box 1306
Anniston, Alabama.

PS - Where Is Don Playing Ball This Year?

Hotel Cromwell 739 South Garland Avenue, Los Angeles 47, California
3-13-53 (excuse the writing)

Dear Patti,

It seems the only way I can contact you, (it's impossible) is to write a few lines. First of all little girl you stood me up the other nite for coffee. I thought we could have a few moments alone to talk. Were you to busey or DID you forget I was waiting? I do want to see you I'm sure if you want too, you can find time to call me at work or drop in to see me (324 So. Main or Madison 63662).

I don't know what people have said to you about me but at least you could let me tell you what I think or how I feel about you.

May I exchange this picture of me which is better than the one you have, for one of you, I've been asking you about if you can't come in to see me give the picture of you to Louie he will give it to me write me a letter if you find time angel, Then till then.

Your's Always Bobbie

21 Gardner St.
Allston, Mass.
Dec. 6, /61.

Dear Patti;

Would you be kind enought to send me a 8"x10" photo of you, I would appreciate it very much. A friend of mine has your pictures, & they are good.

Thank you very much.
Joseph Beade

answered
Jan 30-1962
Send Photo
etc

July 16, 1960
Burbank, Calif.
Dear Patti,

May I said I got your nice note and thank you card it was so nice of you to think of me while you are playing to Seattle Wash. I am so sure the people did go see you at the theatre did enjoy your show. I am sure it was better there. I am sure if I had been there and seen your show I would come back stage to said Hello. You are welcome to the Easter card I am so glad you did like it Patti dear. I did think you are the nicest person in all the world to and I do hope as long as you do live on earth you will always be a big name star and you will star in your Business when some the other shows girls retire and saw their best years. And so you will not only be a big name star but a big headliner and I do hope you will always stay as lovely and pretty and so friendly and nice as you are now. I still have your picture in a frame on the wall at my apt. Well I am so glad I have letter so kind and nice of you I see it because you are the kind of that likes to be so friend.

Yes Patti Dear I do understand you are so busy with your show that (Author's Note: the next line is not readable) you do not have time to write. But it is so nice you do tell me to write you when ever I do this. I had to move from the 160 ½ North Screenland Dr because of the freeway is coming that way, so this is my new address, 125 ½ North Screenland Drive, Burbank, Calif. I like to mail you a little something from Hollywood so you can keep it as a little personal reminder of one of your fans. I still have my fan club card and it does go with me every place I do go Patti Dear.

Well that is all right if you do not have the pin up calendars I do guess the high cost of living (Author's Note: the next several sentences are unreadable)

As a pin up you are a pretty lovely lady Patti and I do said that because I do mean every word of it Dear. I guess it is so hard to find other girls in this business as lovely pretty so nice and so friendly as very good looking as the one the only Patti Waggin is. I am so glad I can not only be a fan of yours but it is nice to have a friend like you write to me. So I will said the next time you are in Los Angeles theatre I will be there and make it my business to come to see you back stage and if I can not get to see you back stage may be you could drop me a card at the hotel you are staying at so I can come by so say Hello. So you just stay right up there on "top" and be a big name star and big headliner in show business Patti. So I will close now and get this off to you.

Your very friendly
Eddie Duncan
125 ½ North Screenland Drive
Burbank, Calif.

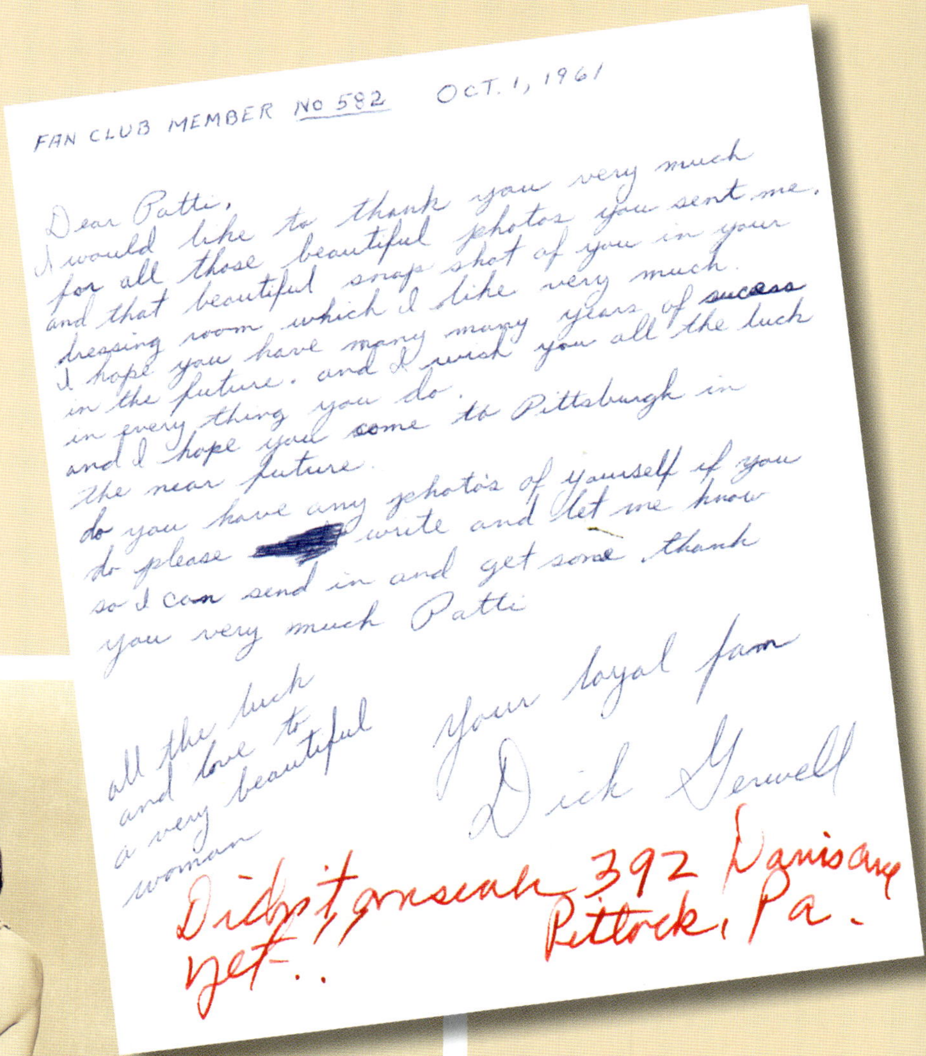

FAN CLUB MEMBER No 582 OCT. 1, 1961

Dear Patti,
I would like to thank you very much
for all those beautiful photos you sent me.
and that beautiful snap shot of you in your
dressing room which I like very much.
I hope you have many many years of success
in the future. and I wish you all the luck
in every thing you do.
and I hope you come to Pittsburgh in
the near future.
do you have any photo's of yourself if you
do please write and let me know
so I can send in and get some. thank
you very much Patti

all the luck
and love to
a very beautiful
woman

Your loyal fan
Dick Gerwell

Didn't answer yet.. 392 Danis ave
Pittock, Pa.

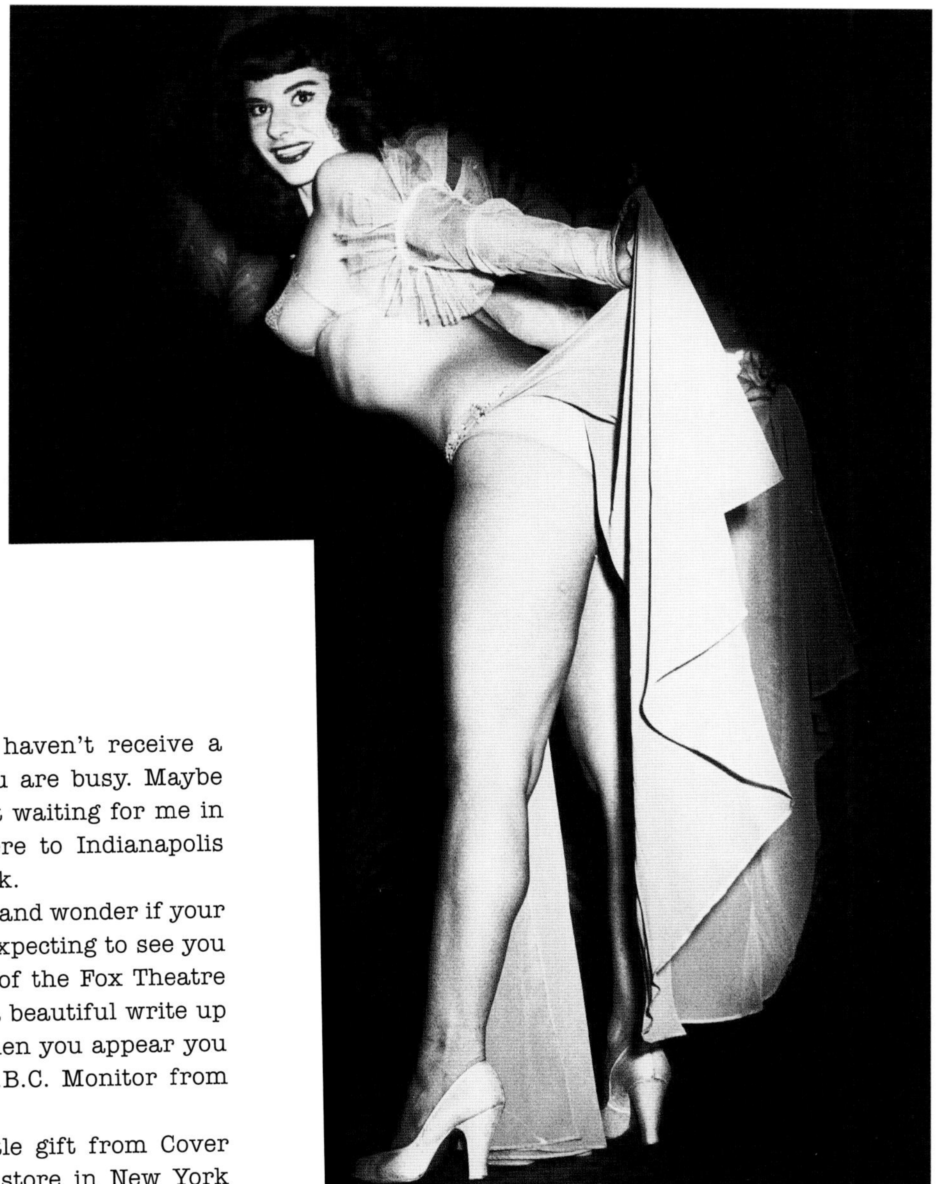

November 25, 1960
Patti Honey,

I have been wondering why I haven't receive a picture of you but then I know you are busy. Maybe when I pickup my mail I will find it waiting for me in Indianapolis as I haven't been there to Indianapolis since Oct 31, but am going this week.

Honey I think of you quite often and wonder if your happy and having good luck. I am expecting to see you once again very soon on the stage of the Fox Theatre in Indianapolis and probable have a beautiful write up of you in the Indianapolis Times when you appear you would make wonderful copy for N.B.C. Monitor from Indianapolis.

Honey I am sending you a little gift from Cover Girl Original Catalog which has a store in New York you probable know the place. You will probable receive it in a couple of weeks. I do want you to accept it as my token of appreciation for having a wonderful pal and friend you will look so sweet in it it's a little dance or pinup suit and I do hope you like it so look for it in about two weeks. So please write and tell me how you feel and are getting along I do want to hear from you real soon. And hope when I get to Indianapolis next week I will find something from you waiting for me at the Post Office as I am so proud of everything you send me and have you for a friend. So bye now Patti honey and I do hope you like my little gift you will look so sweet in it. My little China doll.

All my love,
Johnny

P.S. I haven't forgot the picture of myself you want and someday will surprise you with it Baby darling.

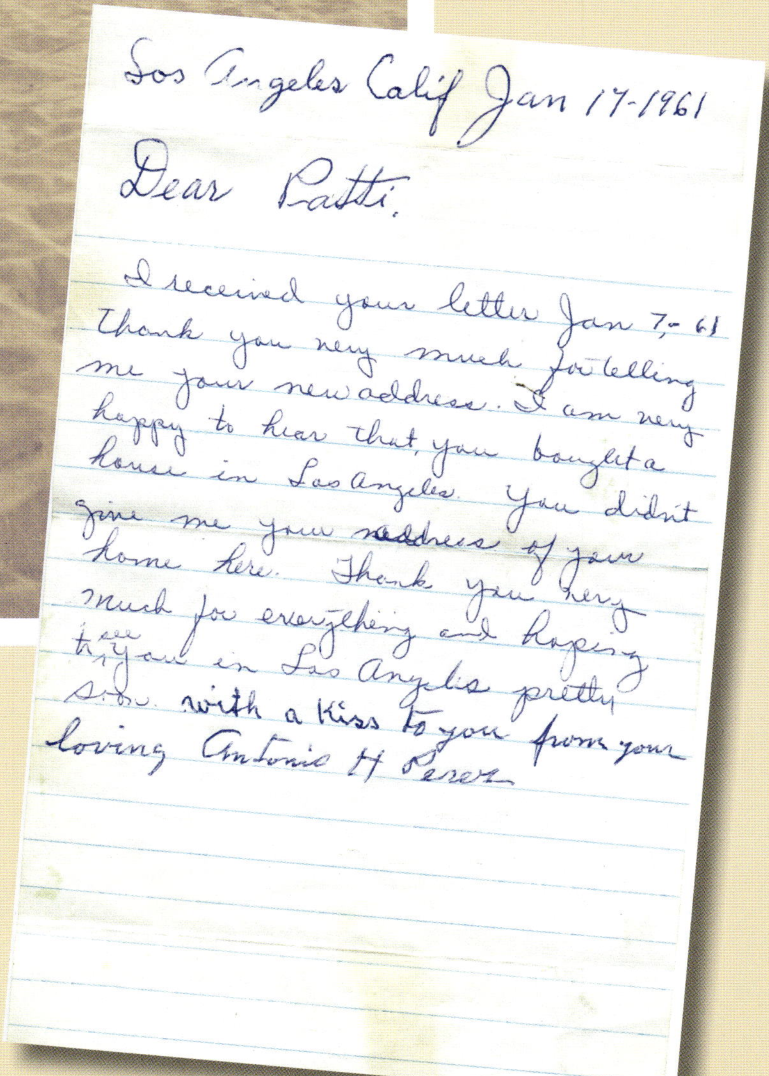

Los Angeles Calif Jan 17-1961

Dear Patti,

I received your letter Jan 7-61 Thank you very much for telling me your new address. I am very happy to hear that, you bought a house in Los Angeles. You didnt give me your address of your home here. Thank you very much for everything and hoping to see you in Los Angeles pretty s.o. with a Kiss to you from your loving Antonio H Perez

Oct. 9, 1960
Dear Patti:

I have been watching the Fox ad in the Indianapolis News, Chili Pepper is there now, but I havent' seen your name. Are you coming if so when?

As my step mother skinned me out of about $40,000 and my heart went bad lungs started to fill up, didn't go anyplace except to bed for about 3 weeks. better now.

I got the pictures you sent last year and I'm fan #272 the pictures were 1 & 5 marked on the back. Thanks

I wonder if you have a picture or can tell me where I can buy one of nude. You – front view – and from top to bottom?

Several of the boys from Clinton saw you at the Fox said you sure were darn good looking and such a nice figure and you sure put on a good show they want to see you when you come back. They think you are a "WOW" – I am the fan who drove almost 150 miles to see the shows 3 to 4 times a mo.

Sincerely,

Clarence Huxford
P.O. Box 391 Clinton, Ina.

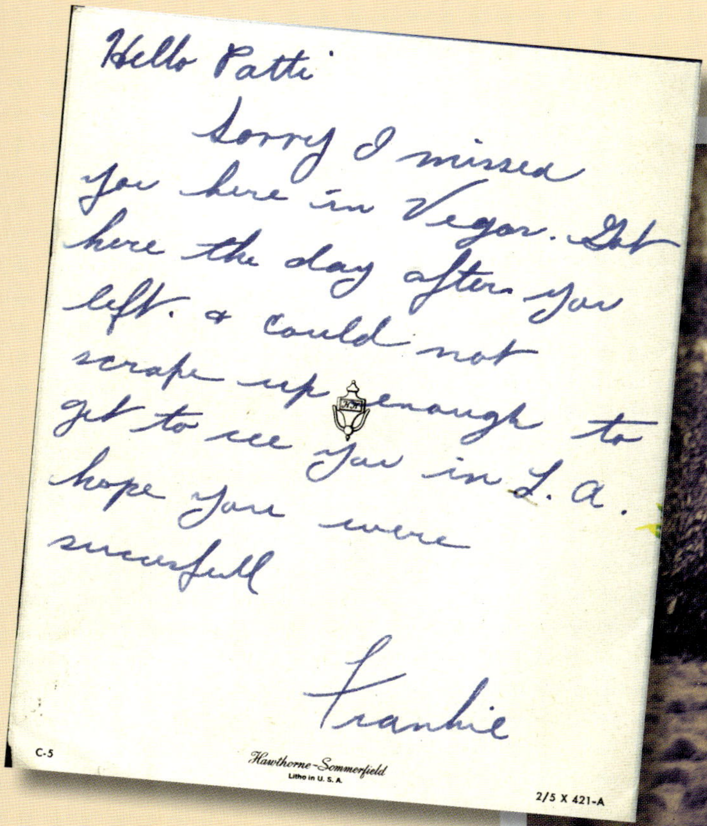
Hello Patti

Sorry I missed you here in Vegas. Got here the day after you left. & could not scrape up enough to get to see you in L.A. hope you were succesfull

Frankie

C-5 Hawthorne-Sommerfield Litho in U.S.A. 2/5 X 421-A

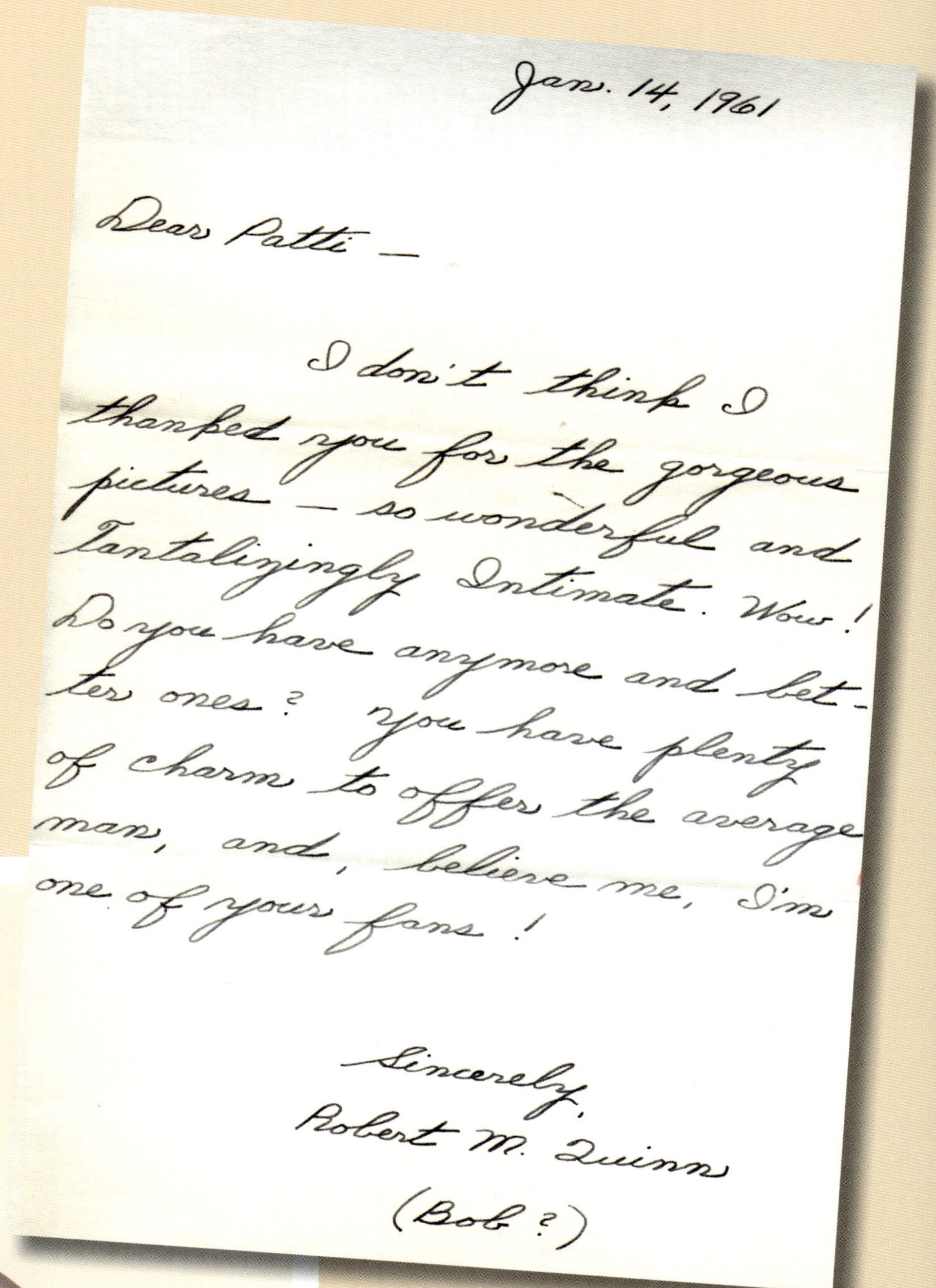

Jan. 14, 1961

Dear Patti –

I don't think I thanked you for the gorgeous pictures – so wonderful and Tantalizingly Intimate. Wow! Do you have anymore and better ones? You have plenty of charm to offer the average man, and, believe me, I'm one of your fans!

Sincerely,
Robert M. Quinn
(Bob?)

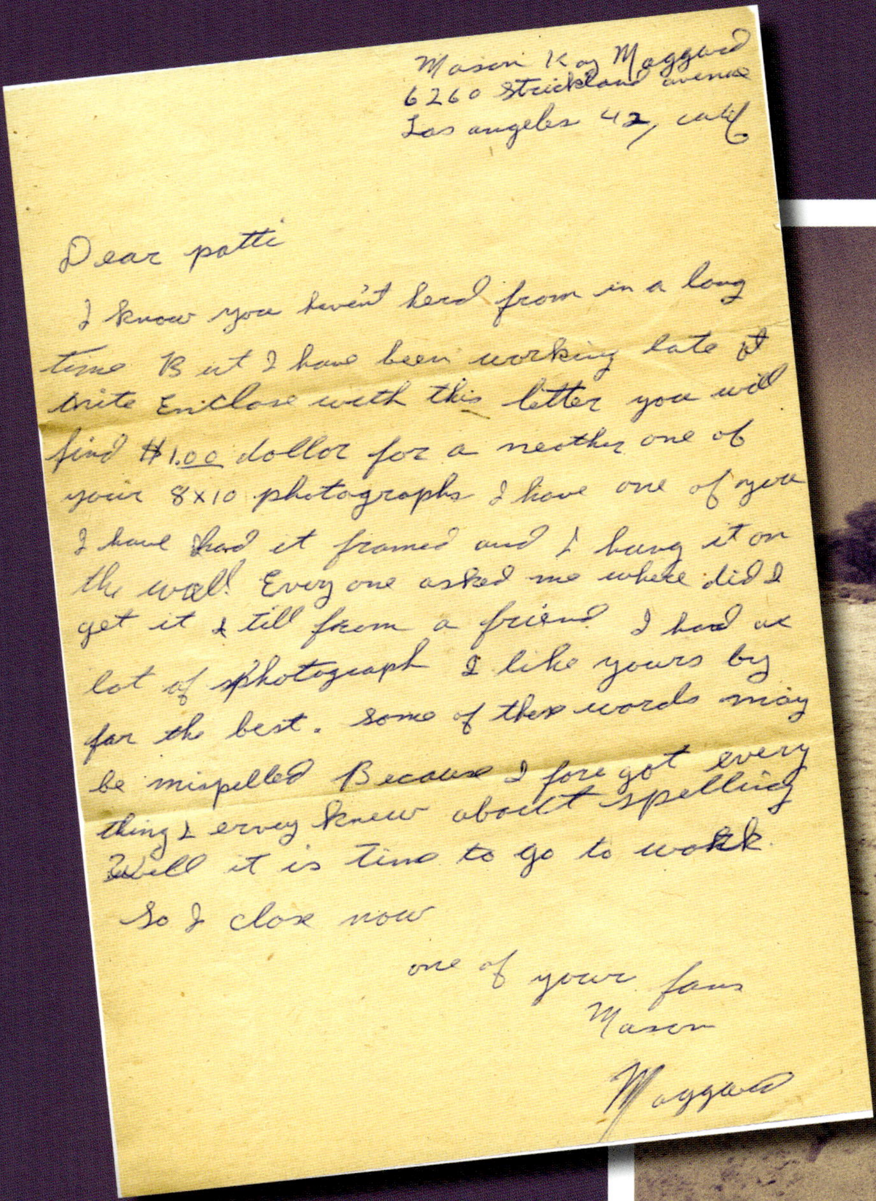

Mason Kay Maggard
6260 Strickland avenue
Los angeles 42, calif

Dear patti

I know you haven't heard from in a long time But I have been working late at nite Enclose with this letter you will find $1.00 dollor for a nother one of your 8x10 photographs I have one of you I have had it framed and I hang it on the wall! Every one asked me where did I get it I till from a friend I had a lot of photograph I like yours by far the best. some of thes words may be mispelled Because I fore got every thing I ever knew about spelling Well it is time to go to work.

So I close now

one of your fans
Mason
Maggard

Tuesday 16 May 1961
Miss Patti Waggin
15718 Index
Granada Hills, California

Dear Patti,

I have just received the 2 very nice signed photos – and the note from you –and want to write you right back to let you know how much I enjoyed and appreciated hearing from you. I had written to you a couple of times in Indianapolis – and realize you are quite a busy Young Lady so it is a Real Thrill to correspond with you. As you probably know I also "follow" Donnies Career closely and religiously through the Sporting News. I think I will wirite him again in a few days – he had told me quite a long while ago that you would send me some signed photos. I had been anxiously looking forward to receiving them and am real thrilled. And pleased to add them to my collection.

I was also surprised to learn you had bought a new home in Granada Hills – it's a beautiful section and I know you are both proud of it. You see I know quite a bit about that part of the country. I lived in Whittier, California for a little over a year. In fact I have been back in Anniston only about a year now. Incidently I just missed meeting you when you had an engagement in a club in Los Angeles. I forget the name of the club but as I remember it was around 6th & Main and you had Top Billing then oh, about 2 ½ years or so ago. I went down to introduce myself to you and the girl in the office told me you had just left and it was your last performance. I sure hated to miss you and didn't know where you were staying so it was just impossible for me to find you. I don't know what "type of life" you live "on the road" but was hoping we could have met and had dinner together and talked over "common interests." If you were alone, I know how that can be in Los Angeles with no real friends. I was there for a couple of months without my wifeand even with all it's excitements and activities I could not satisfy my missing link – even though it's a big wide awake place, one can get lonely there. Someday, Somewhere though I hope to meet you and Don both – you seem to be swell people. I wish you both the very best that life has to offer.

I hope you will have time to write me again and I would like you to sign the 3 cards enclosed

1. Patti Waggin
2. Pattie Waggin Rudolph
3. Your real Name (I assume Pattie Waggin is a stage name)

Give my very best Personal Regards to Don. And wish him luck with the Indians.
With continued Best Personal Regards,
And Hoping to hear from you again Real Soon.
I am, very sincerely your friend,

T. Roy Pitts
P.O. Box 1306
Anniston, Alabama

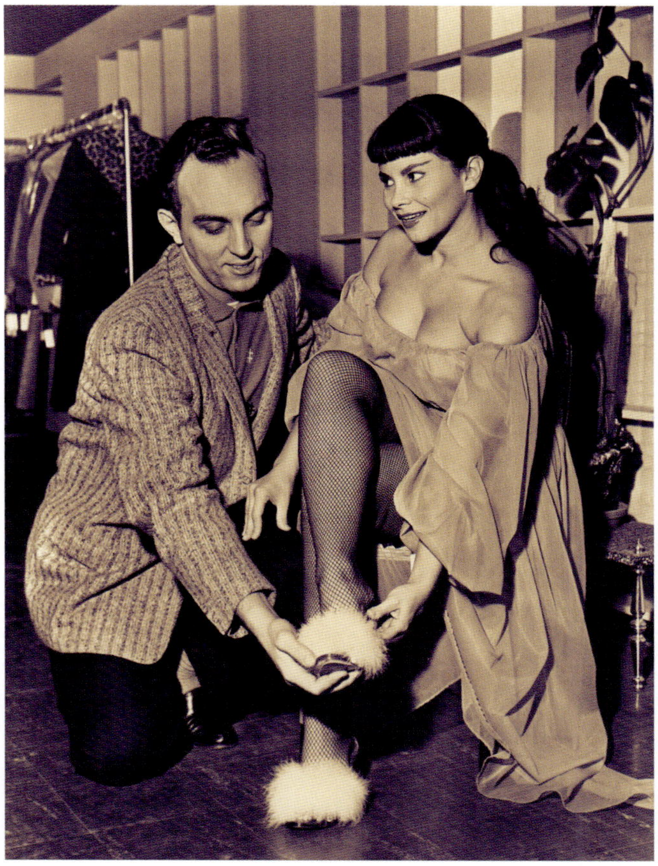

SAVOY
BURLESK ON STAGE
"PATTI WAGGIN"
BURLESK ON STAGE
"PATTI WAGGIN"
PATTI WAGGIN
PATTI WAGGIN
NO PARKING BETWEEN SIGNS

Domino
SIERRA
Interpretive Dancer
RAVEENA
Queen of Pantomime
Starring
PATTIE WAGGIN
THE CO-ED
WITH THE EDUCATED TORSO!
The TOKYE TRIO
DAVE TOWNSEND
Orchestra
Nitely
Excellent
DINNERS
FROM 5 P.M.
MODERATELY PRICED
THE FINEST
ENTERTAINMENT
AT ALL TIMES
FINE MUSIC
FOR YOUR
Dancing & Listening Pleasure

CHRIS SENAKOS

Chris

The Co-Ed With the Educated Torso

The Chico State Years

Chico State College, long designated a party school in some circles, gained one of their livlier co-eds in Patti. Whether Patti signed up because of the school's reputation or because she was developing a relationship with Bill Brownell, Chico's Indian motorcycle distributor, and wanted to be close by is a subject open for debate. While attending college at Chico, Patti appeared in a student stage production of Pinocchio. However, she quickly discovered she had a real affinity for dancing lessons and took to them with enthusiasm. Encouraged by her dance instructor, Patti experimented, adding athletic twists to classic dance steps to create a lively performance sure to show off her style and her form in later years and get those fan letters started.

While at Chico, Patti got her first break, taking her first steps into the world of burlesque. She and a friend went to a club in San Francisco where there was a chance to perform. Patti quickly discovered she had a talent for stripping and enjoyed the work. Patti's friend, although quite good herself, did not return. Her husband was not fond of idea of his wife performing in a strip club, and he was not enthusiastic about Patti either. Undeterred, Patti stripped her way through college in some of the Bay area's rougher, sleazier clubs. Bill Brownell was fine with the arrangement as it kept his new wife happy.

In time, Patti was ready to take her act on the road. In the late 1940s, Patti signed on as a dancer with the Hollywood Debs and headed off with the all-girl group for an extended stay in Honolulu, Hawaii.

Meanwhile, Bill Brownell stayed in Chico and the marriage ended. Patti kept the Brownell name until 1955, however, when she married Don Rudolph. Her marriage license even states that Patricia Brownell was marrying Don Rudolph.

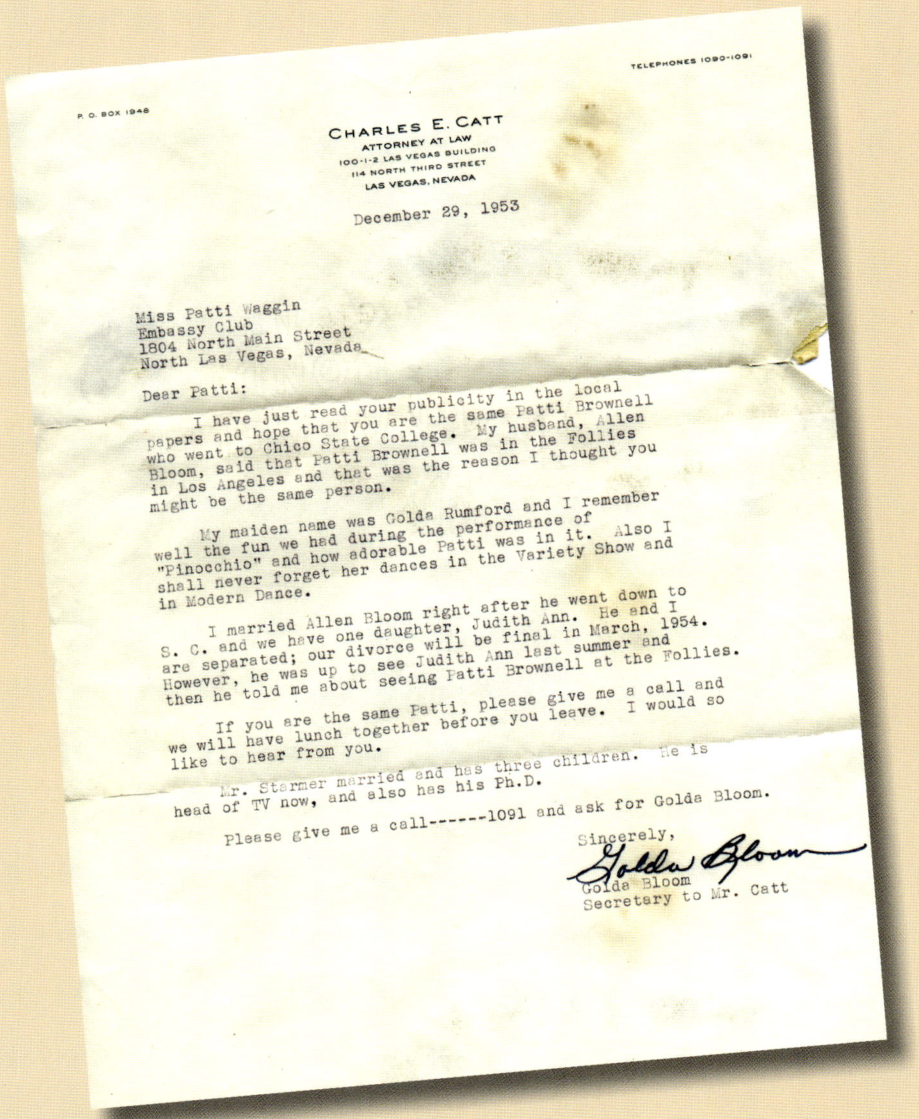

P. O. BOX 1948

TELEPHONES 1090-1091

CHARLES E. CATT
ATTORNEY AT LAW
100-1-2 LAS VEGAS BUILDING
114 NORTH THIRD STREET
LAS VEGAS, NEVADA

December 29, 1953

Miss Patti Waggin
Embassy Club
1804 North Main Street
North Las Vegas, Nevada

Dear Patti:

I have just read your publicity in the local papers and hope that you are the same Patti Brownell who went to Chico State College. My husband, Allen Bloom, said that Patti Brownell was in the Follies in Los Angeles and that was the reason I thought you might be the same person.

My maiden name was Golda Rumford and I remember well the fun we had during the performance of "Pinocchio" and how adorable Patti was in it. Also I shall never forget her dances in the Variety Show and in Modern Dance.

I married Allen Bloom right after he went down to S. C. and we have one daughter, Judith Ann. He and I are separated; our divorce will be final in March, 1954. However, he was up to see Judith Ann last summer and then he told me about seeing Patti Brownell at the Follies.

If you are the same Patti, please give me a call and we will have lunch together before you leave. I would so like to hear from you.

Mr. Starmer married and has three children. He is head of TV now, and also has his Ph.D.

Please give me a call------1091 and ask for Golda Bloom.

Sincerely,

Golda Bloom
Golda Bloom
Secretary to Mr. Catt

Sept 21, 1952

Dear Patti,

I was in Los Angeles this past week and I had the occasion to catch your beautiful dance at the New Follies Theatre. I feel that you are a lovely welcome attraction to the art of strippers. I have seen them in Paris, Rome, London, New York, Dallas, Cleveland and Philadelphia but quite a few were old; and how shall I say it, shopworn looking. Yours was a fresh vibrant beauty that helps life a bit easier to endure. At first you might say I am an old man from this letter but I am only 26. The army provided a lot of transportation.

I see you once went to Chico State. Correct me if I'm wrong. Fresno State our local college has played Chico many times and I once went to a dance there with a girl who looked a lot like you. She had the grace and symmetry of you and even your figure. Need I say I cannot at the moment recall her name. But up until last week I had not enjoyed an evening more until I saw you at the Follies. Maybe it was you.

And so I make a simple request. All I ask is a picture or two of your lovely figure, particularly your torso, and also a kind word or two in a note of which will be appreciated. If a correspondence is wished I am your man. I enclose $1.00 to help defray the cost of the photos and I will longingly wait for your letter.

I remain obediently yours
Herbert Morrison c/o Gen. Del. Fresno

At Chico State, Patti Brownell took part in all sorts of activities, including baseball and basketball. This is where the co-ed began developing her unique athletic style of dance and where she began grooming what would be her look on stage.

Probably the rarest of all Patricia Brownell photos is the school portrait shot. She missed her college yearbook with the exception of a few group shots.

Above with new husband Bill Brownell and friend, shortly after Patti and Bill tied the knot. Below, Patti gets a starring role in the Chico State performance of Pinocchio. She would write later it was a thrill performing on stage.

Pin-Up and Don't Let the Boys DOWN

Although Bettie Grable was every soldier's dream in World War II, Patti Waggin had G.I. tongues waggin' in Korea. During the Korean conflict, Patti was at the top of her game. She was a headliner from the American Heartland to Vegas and on to Los Angeles. Soldiers stationed everywhere around the globe wrote to Patti.

Whenever Patti was performing within 150 miles of the ubiquitous American military bases, soldiers flocked out to see her. Everybody from high ranking colonels to cooks came out to see Patti and none of them could resist writing her letters.

Soldiers wrote asking for pin-ups, asking for Patti's hand in marriage, or asking for what was on every young, healthy, red-blooded American male's mind. In later years, fans who followed baseball would ask about Don's career as well ... but then would add wistfully, "I wish you were single."

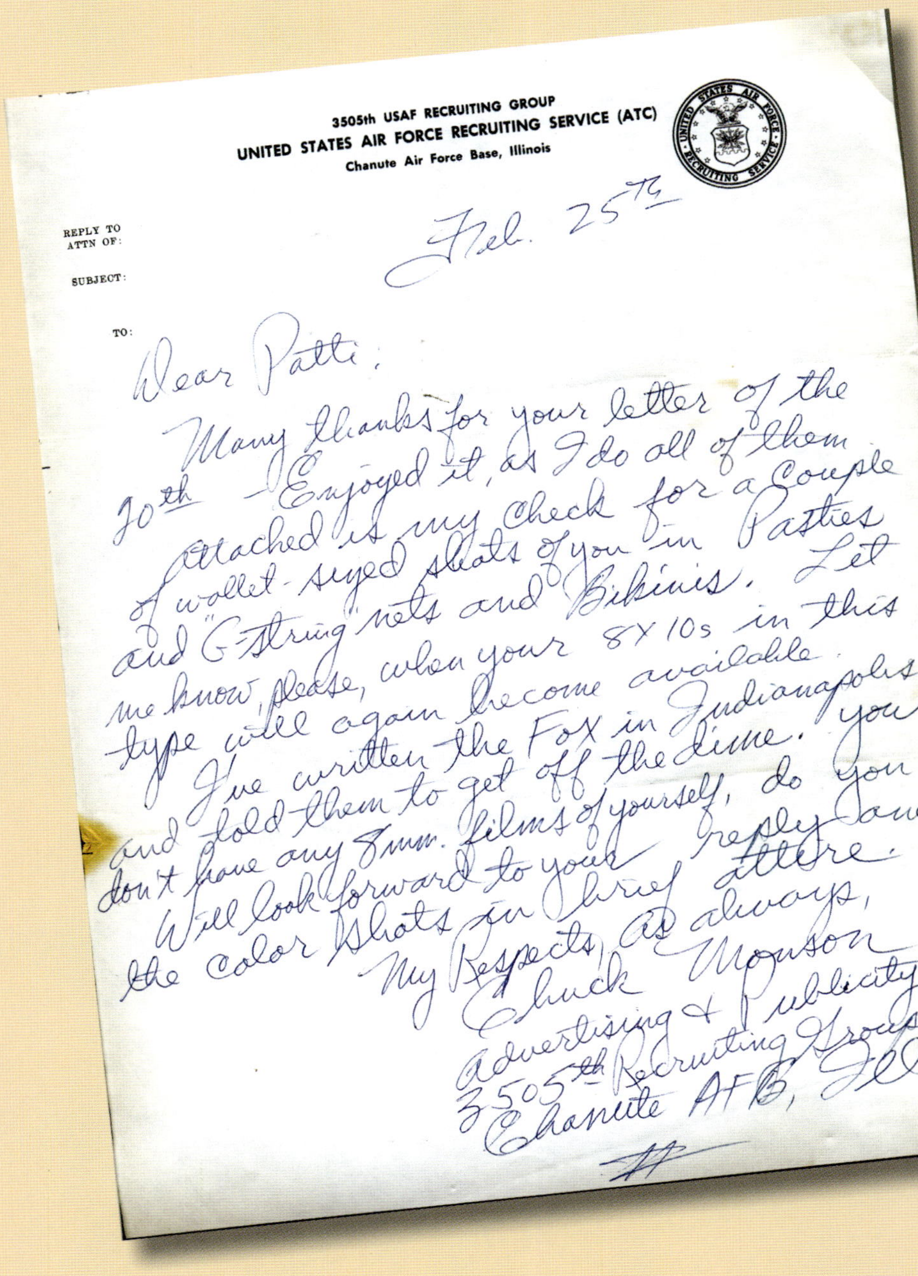

3505th USAF RECRUITING GROUP
UNITED STATES AIR FORCE RECRUITING SERVICE (ATC)
Chanute Air Force Base, Illinois

REPLY TO ATTN OF:

SUBJECT:

TO:

Feb. 25th

Dear Patti:

Many thanks for your letter of the 20th. Enjoyed it, as I do all of them. Attached is my check for a couple of wallet-sized shots of you in Pasties and "G-String" nets and Bikinis. Let me know, please, when your 8X10s in this type will again become available.

I've written the Fox in Indianapolis and told them to get off the dime. You don't have any 8mm. films of yourself, do you?

Will look forward to your reply and the color shots in brief attire.

My Respects, as always,
Chuck Monson
Advertising & Publicity
3505th Recruiting Group
Chanute AFB, Ill.

September 11, 1952
North Korea

Hello Pattie

I seen a picture of you today and haven't been able to think straight since! You took my breath away and my heart just won't stand still.

I should be rotating in about 3 months (I have been here 14 already) and believe me I will be at the Spanish Village to see the breath taking beauty whose picture sent my heart racing.

Really Pattie I think you are just tops in every way and I would like very much to have your friendship.

Pattie forgive me for writing to you like this but Honey I have never seen anyone I liked more than you.

Today for a change a lot of mail came in. See what a big difference a letter can make. There was just about a letter for everyone! Everybody was going around with a big smile, laughing, joking. It really was great cause that don't happen in a place like this very often. I'm thinking how happy I would have been if I would have receive a letter from you. I know you are very busy but if you ever care to win a slave for life and lose me a heart forever just write to me!

I would also like so very much to have a personally autographed picture from you to me. Believe me I would treasure it for the rest of my life! Pattie are you married? Also in the way of question – what is the measurements of that wonderful body of yours?

Pattie I would like to know you better all about yourself, your career ect. How about it – would you be so wonderful and thrill me with a letter and a picture!! Please do!

I will close this letter to the most thrilling Girl I have ever seen. I hope to get an answer real soon.

Please write
I love you
Wally Spencer
PFC Robert W. Spencer
Author's Note: He puts in his military serial number here
KMAG – 2nd ROK Corps
APO 102
S.F. Calif.

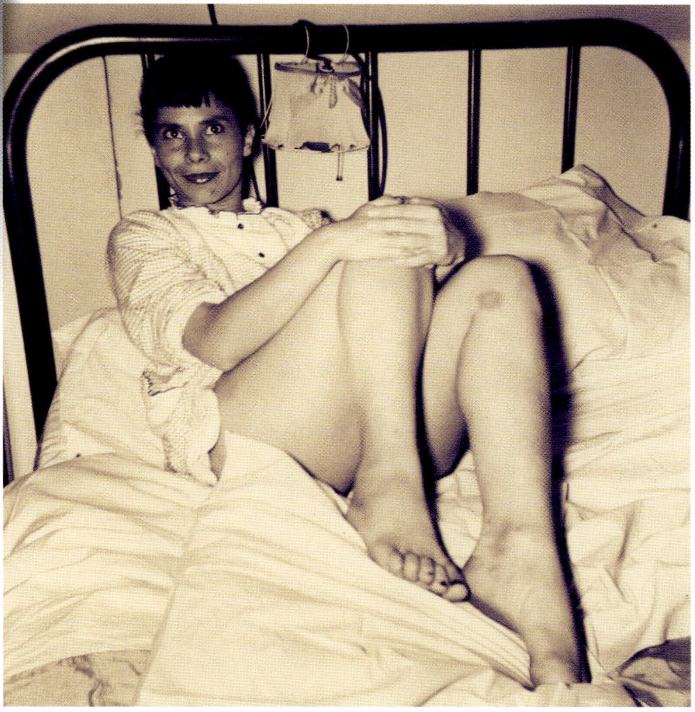

OPEN ALL NITE
TEASING
SIZZLING
TANTALIZING
The Inimitable
PATTI WAGGIN
in A PARISIAN PICKUP
TOO HOT
TO
HANDLE

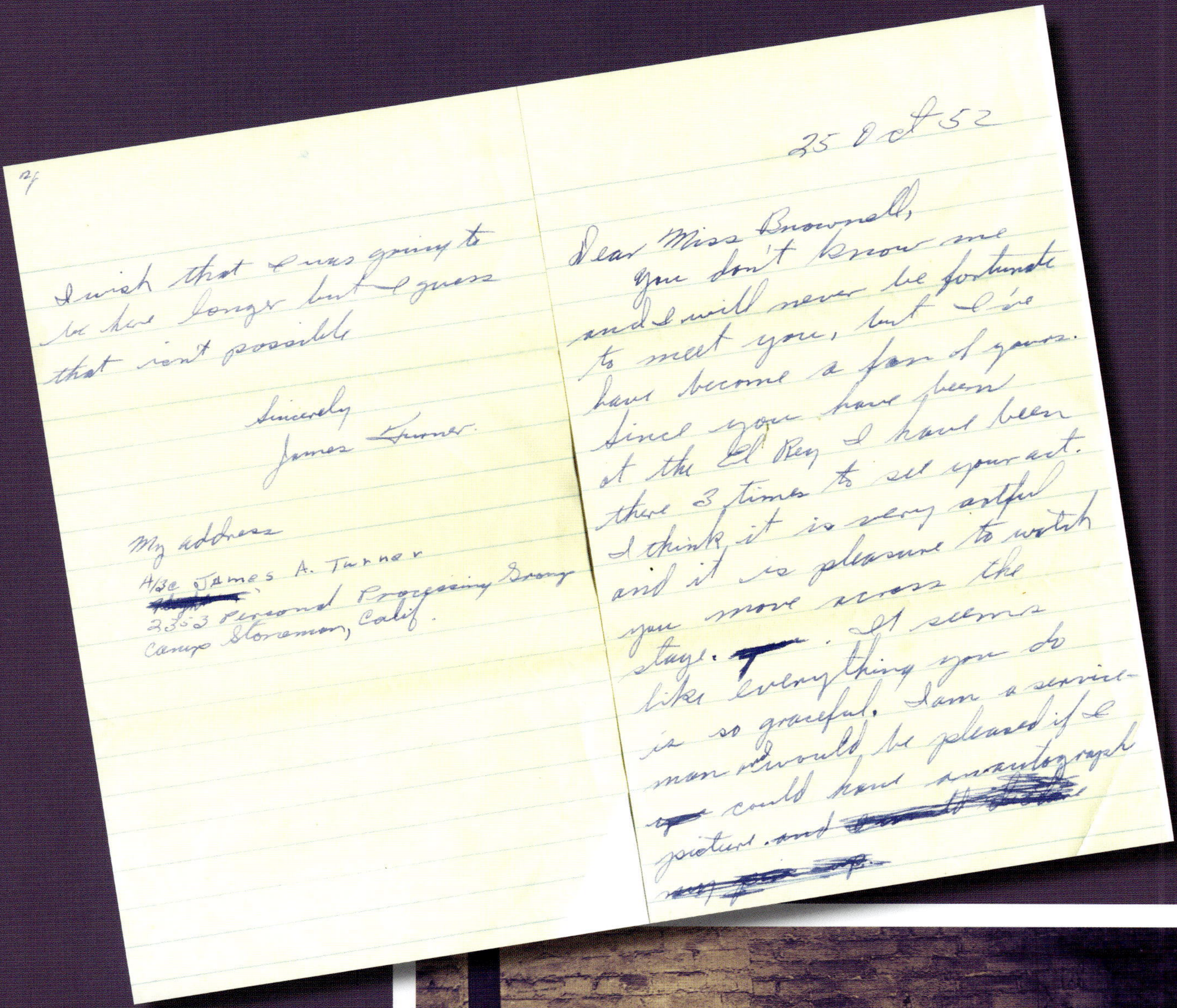

25 Oct 52

Dear Miss Brownell,

You don't know me and I will never be fortunate to meet you, but I've have become a fan of yours. Since you have been at the El Rey I have been there 3 times to see your act. I think it is very artful and it is pleasure to watch you move across the stage. It seems like everything you do is so graceful. I am a service-man I would be pleased if I could have an autograph picture. and

2

I wish that I was going to be here longer but I guess that isn't possible.

Sincerely
James Turner.

My address
A/3c James A. Turner
2353 Personnel Processing Group
Camp Stoneman, Calif.

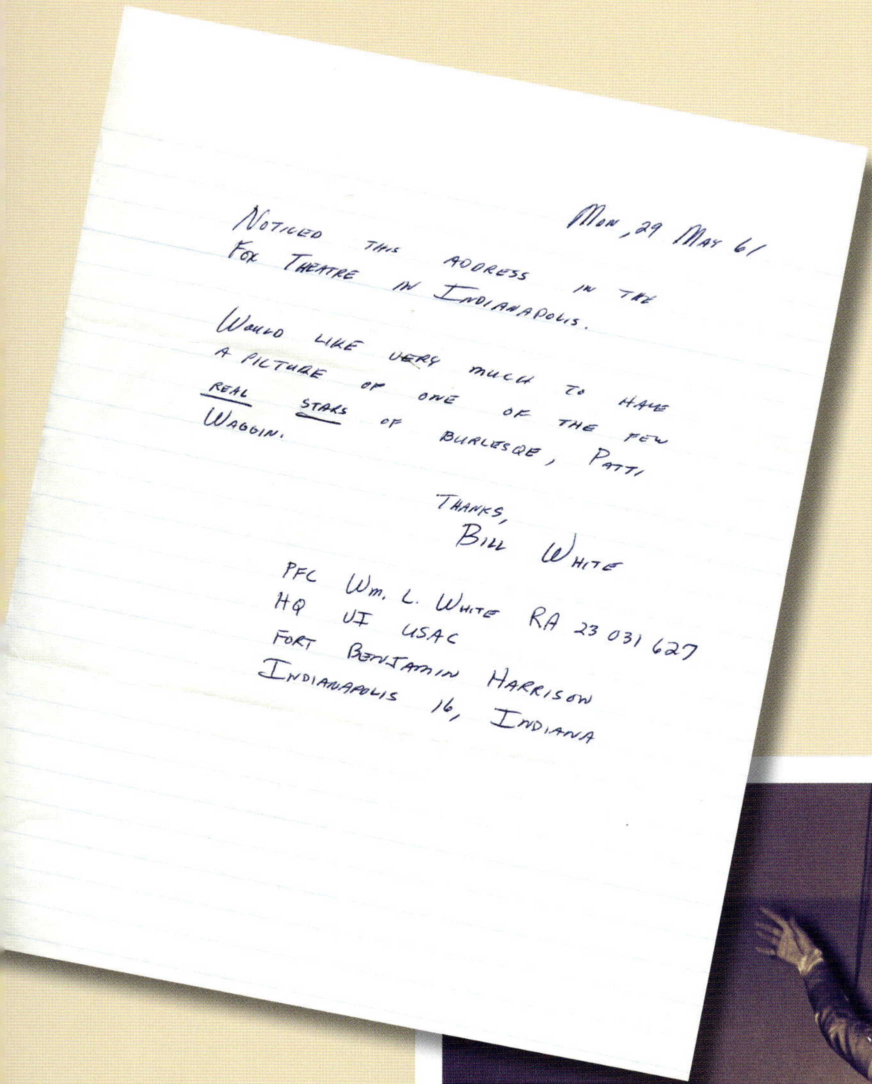

Mon, 29 May 61

Noticed this address in the Fox Theatre in Indianapolis.

Would like very much to have a picture of one of the few real stars of burlesqe, Patti Waggin.

Thanks,
Bill White

PFC Wm. L. White RA 23 031 627
HQ UI USAC
Fort Benjamin Harrison
Indianapolis 16, Indiana

ATED TORSO
the D
GIRLS
HOT DOGS
BURRITOS
TACOS
TAMALE & CHILI
Sandwiches
PATTI
WAGGIN
NOW PLAYING
NEXT COMPLETE
STAGE SHOW
Patti
WAGGIN
TAQUIT
10
TACOS • BURRIT
MENUDO-HOY

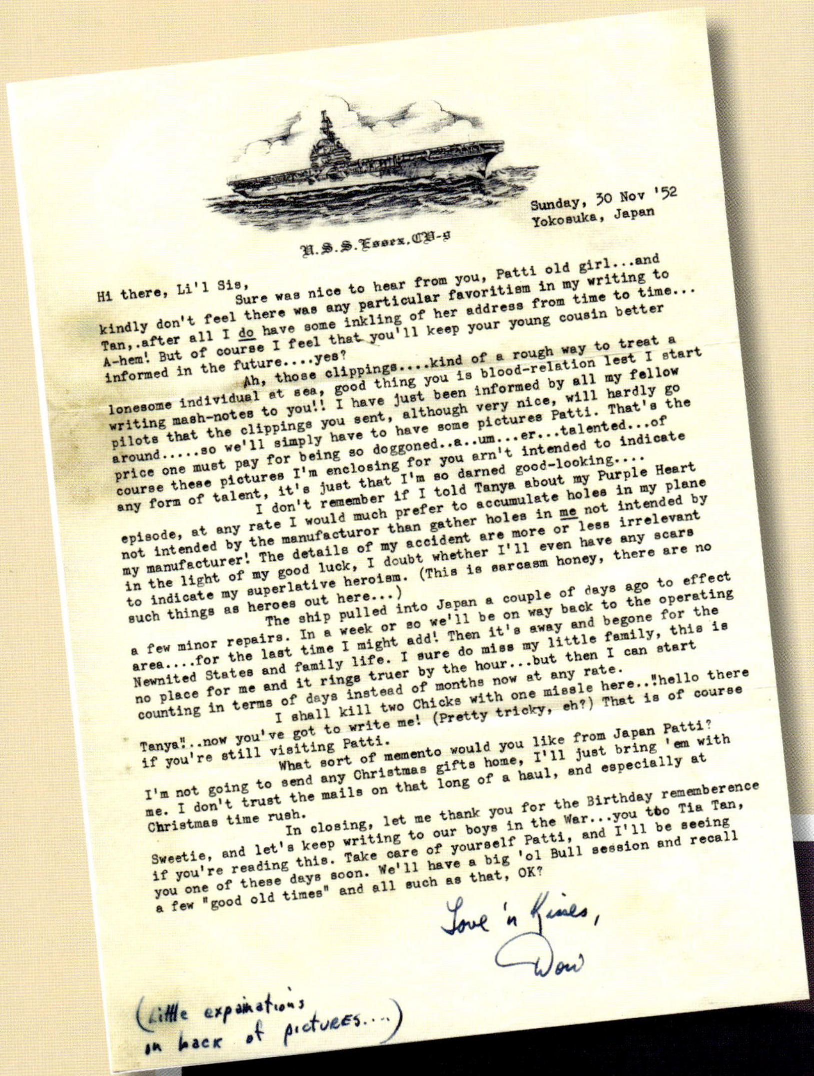

Sunday, 30 Nov '52
Yokosuka, Japan

U.S.S. Essex, CV-9

Hi there, Li'l Sis,
Sure was nice to hear from you, Patti old girl...and
kindly don't feel there was any particular favoritism in my writing to
Tan,.after all I do have some inkling of her address from time to time...
A-hem! But of course I feel that you'll keep your young cousin better
informed in the future....yes?
Ah, those clippings....kind of a rough way to treat a
lonesome individual at sea, good thing you is blood-relation lest I start
writing mash-notes to you!! I have just been informed by all my fellow
pilots that the clippings you sent, although very nice, will hardly go
around.....so we'll simply have to have some pictures Patti. That's the
price one must pay for being so doggoned..a..um...er...talented...of
course these pictures I'm enclosing for you arn't intended to indicate
any form of talent, it's just that I'm so darned good-looking....
I don't remember if I told Tanya about my Purple Heart
episode, at any rate I would much prefer to accumulate holes in my plane
not intended by the manufacturor than gather holes in me not intended by
my manufacturer! The details of my accident are more or less irrelevant
in the light of my good luck, I doubt whether I'll even have any scars
to indicate my superlative heroism. (This is sarcasm honey, there are no
such things as heroes out here...)
The ship pulled into Japan a couple of days ago to effect
a few minor repairs. In a week or so we'll be on way back to the operating
area....for the last time I might add! Then it's away and begone for the
Newnited States and family life. I sure do miss my little family, this is
no place for me and it rings truer by the hour...but then I can start
counting in terms of days instead of months now at any rate.
I shall kill two Chicks with one missle here.."hello there
Tanya"..now you've got to write me! (Pretty tricky, eh?) That is of course
if you're still visiting Patti.
What sort of memento would you like from Japan Patti?
I'm not going to send any Christmas gifts home, I'll just bring 'em with
me. I don't trust the mails on that long of a haul, and especially at
Christmas time rush.
In closing, let me thank you for the Birthday rememberence
Sweetie, and let's keep writing to our boys in the War...you too Tia Tan,
if you're reading this. Take care of yourself Patti, and I'll be seeing
you one of these days soon. We'll have a big 'ol Bull session and recall
a few "good old times" and all such as that, OK?

Love 'n Kisses,
Don

(little explanations
on back of pictures...)

United States Marine Corps
First Marine Division FMF
Camp Pendleton, California

Dear Patti

I was very shocked and very pleased to receive your little note today. I thought my letter to you would be completely ignored. From the Picture that I saw of you you didn't seem like that kind of a person.

I thought I'd write you a little line even though you probably won't have time to answer this one, but with you away from home, I imagine you'd like to hear from someone. I hope someone will forward it to you.

California has been real nice the past few weeks except for the past two days when the heat got fairly unbearable. But it should cool of a little in the next few days.

I know weather isn't a real pleasant subject but I can't think of too much to say right now.

I hope you are enjoying yourself in South America? Are you working or taking a long vacation?

I'd like to hear from you if you get the time if not I'll be looking for your letter in April.

Well I'd better close for now. I'll be waiting for your return to the States. Have a good time the rest of your trip.

Love Dave

My address:

Cpl. David J. Ohmsted
M.P. Co Hq. Bn
1st Mar. Div. F.M.F.
Camp Pendleton, Calif.

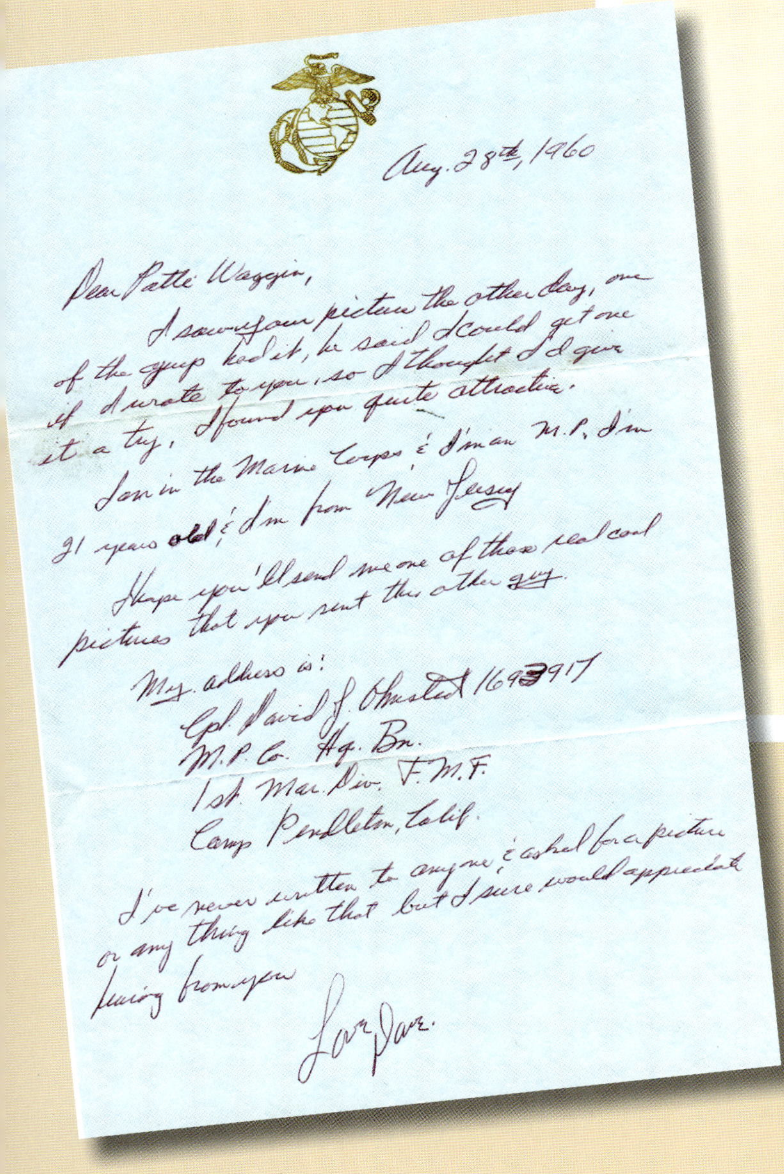
Aug. 28th, 1960

Dear Pattie Waggin,

I saw your picture the other day, one of the guys had it, he said I could get one if I wrote to you, so I thought I'd give it a try. I found you quite attractive.

I am in the Marine Corps & I'm an M.P. I'm 21 years old & I'm from New Jersey

Hope you'll send me one of those real cool pictures that you sent the other guy.

My address is:
Cpl. David J. Olmsted 1693917
M.P. Co. Hq. Bn.
1st. Mar. Div. F.M.F.
Camp Pendleton, Calif.

I've never written to anyone & asked for a picture or anything like that but I sure would appreciate hearing from you

Love Dave.

United States Marine Corps
Sept 19, 1952

Dear Patti,

I know this sound a wee bit silly but I caught you show the other night and writing to request if you would bother to send me a nice pin up photo of yourselfe as I admired you very much and if it isn't too much trouble would you please audograph it to and Thanks a million.

a everlasting admier,
Bill

My address
PFC Thomas W. Rice
Division Disbursing office (14-Mail)
HQ CO. HQ Bn 3rd Marine Div. FMF
Camp Pendletion California
Thanks a Lot

Miss Patti Bonell
c/o Spanish Village
San Francisco, Calif:-

Dear Patti:—

We of the 45th Division Air Section are badly in need of some pin-ups to bolster our morale!

I have heard that you are one of the prettiest show girls in San Francisco, so am taking the liberty to request some pin ups from you. —Autographed please!?

CAPT. LOEHR RIGBY
45th DIV. AIR SECT.
A.P.O. 86 c/o P.M.
SAN FRANCISCO, CALIF.

Sincerely
Loehr Rigby
Capt artillery.

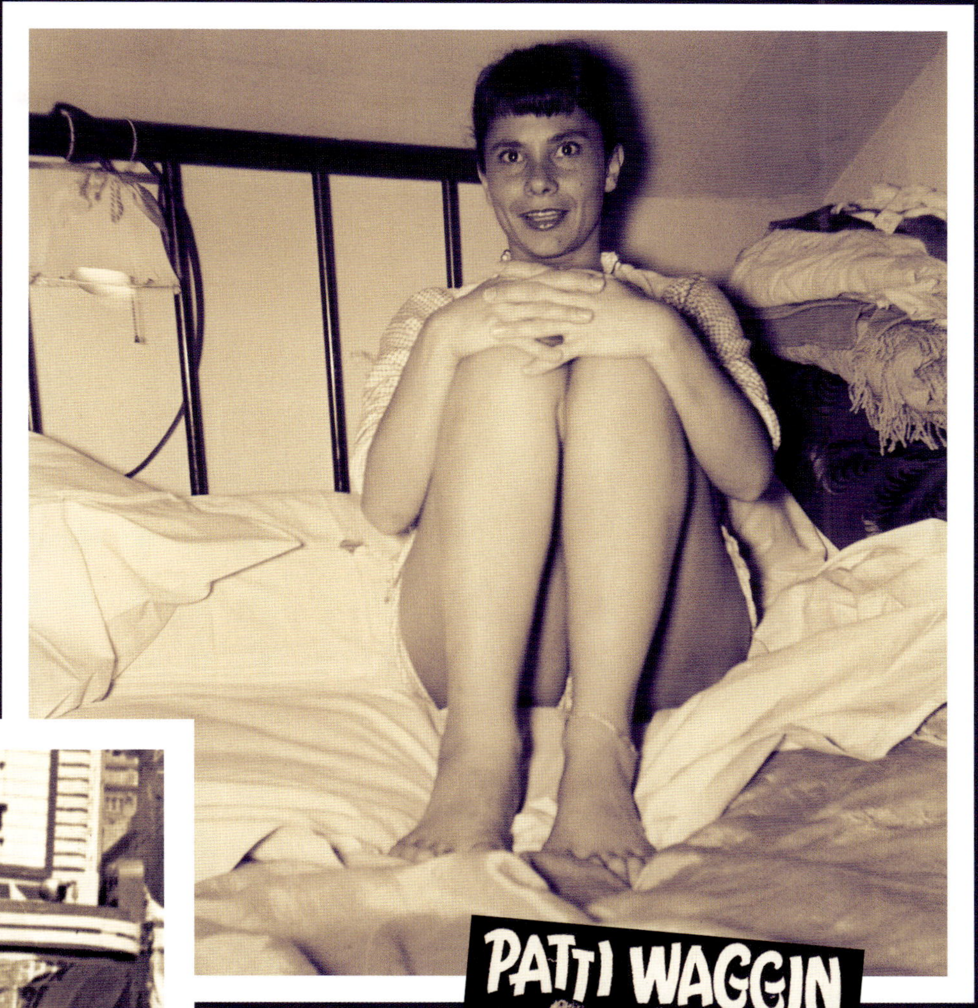

FOR HIRE"
MAE WEST
NIGHT"

PATTI WAGGIN
"The Sex-Comp Doll"
On Stage-In Person
March
2ND
OAKLAND
EL REY Burlesk
1956 MARCH 1956
SUN MON TUE WED THU FRI SAT
1 2 3
4 5 6 7 8 9 10
11 12 13 14 15 16 17
18 19 20 21 22 23 24
25 26 27 28 29 30 31

Sunday AM

Dear Patti,

One of my two life long ambitions has been realized. I saw you last night with clothes on. Last Saturday on the 9th of February I had to get my lonesome fired up and yesterday I had to work. So I went to your show last night. I forgot to mail a letter I had and was putting in the mail box at 7 & Main after 1st shows when you came by. I was standing right beside you while you waited for the red light to change. You went over to the P.E. Drug Store, bought some cleanex or something, stopped to talk a minute with the man that sells newspapers. Baby I wasn't spying on you really. Only I want to meet you so bad. You had on a long light blue coat & I think red shoes. You know men are bashful anyway, compared to women and I am the worst of the lot and last night I needed a haircut, I hadn't shaved since moving and worst of all I had green onions for dinner. I will never touch them again. I never dreamed of seeing you except on the stage.

Patti for anybody raised like I was it is hard to speak to a girl on the street who don't know you. I am sitting in the car in the parking lot of the Campus Theatre at Santa Monica & Vermont writing this. It is 10:00. Mr. Hall talks at 11:00. One of your notices said you started to be a teacher. You must have had a lot of it. I know you would enjoy Mr. Hall. Next Sunday is his last lecture till in April. He goes to New York for two weeks. If you could put your head on my shoulder and go to sleep. No? Patti studying Philosophy for a long time gives you a kind of a sixth sense and I have always been very intuitional. So I am going to tell you something about yourself.

Next Summer, June, July & August, a big change is coming in your life. Maybe you are going to have a terrific love affair. Maybe you will get married but anyway things are going to change. Maybe you will give up Burlesque, I don't know just what is going to happen but I do know there is a major changing coming in your life. You don't do anything half way, every thing you do is all out. That is your nature.

Only the best is good enough for you. Today is my birthday last year on my birthday I sent you roses and you looked sour & glum through the whole shows. I will never be happy till I found out why? I am going to send you a little present for my birthday. You see that Chili Pepper & Suzie has me worried. I wonder if you won't be there next weekend. I thought you were taking Loreli's place, she played almost all last year at the Follies.

I just came out of the lecture. I wish you could have been there you would have understood what I have been telling you about your inner beauty which never shone so brightly as last night in front of the P.E. Building. You were <u>so sweet</u> but looked winsome and kinda lonesome someway. I never realized before what a <u>little</u> girl you are you would not come up to my shoulder. I I never see you again I will always remember you as you stood talking to the Newsman. I dreamed about you last night. For me not a very satisfactory one. It went like this.

"There used to be a man in your audience who was important to you but now you have forgotten all about him."

Patti you are not shallow like some of the people around you and you have a beautiful soul, I wish you could understand these things. I know why you are in Burlesque. Do you? And the reason is wonderful & beautiful but it must only be a sojourn in your life. Patti take our money and buy yourself a present from me a night gown, slip or a pair of apricot colored panties with blue bows on the sides. Use it for costume jewelry or strings on anything in any way. I wish our paths would really cross. Maybe who knows! There are a lot of things I could tell you I think would interest you. For instances what actually happens when one person falls for another. Few people know this but I do. Patti if I ever see you alone again and say Patti this is Bill, are you going to call the cops? Might as well say love from Bill. If I denied it you would know it wasn't so – will you see me some time baby doll.

Author's Note: Bill never signed his name and sent an envelope with no return address and a Los Angeles Postmark, March 8, 1955. It should also be noted he sent similar letters later.

The Artist in Everyone

Patti's admirers were often inspired to immortalize her in ink or on canvas, creating images of her more memorable poses and performances from memory or, as Tony Skau regularly did, from her publicity stills. Tony would create what he considered artful renderings of Patti and send them on for her review.

From his letters, we learn that Tony sent his renderings two at a time, with considerable frequency. Apparently, prior to the letters and images captured here, Tony had used his imagination to create nude renderings of Patti. Considering the strength of Tony's declaration that he would never send another nude, one can imagine Patti's response to these original works had been less than favorable.

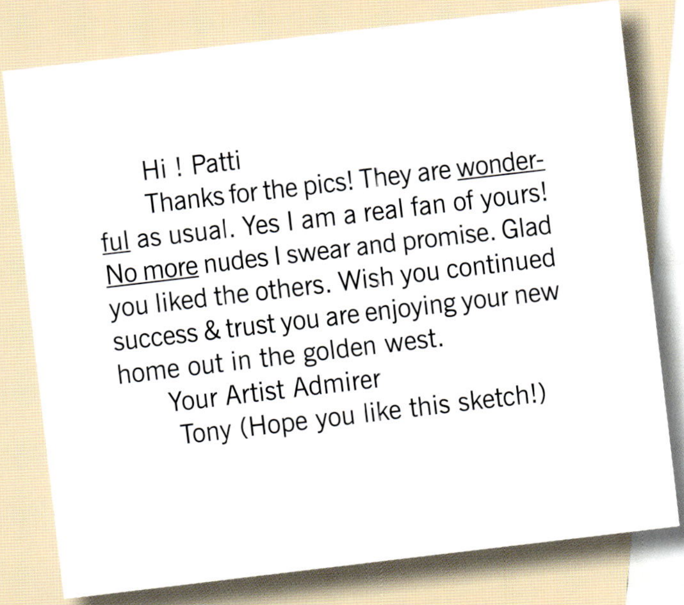

Hi ! Patti

Thanks for the pics! They are wonderful as usual. Yes I am a real fan of yours! No more nudes I swear and promise. Glad you liked the others. Wish you continued success & trust you are enjoying your new home out in the golden west.

Your Artist Admirer

Tony (Hope you like this sketch!)

Hi! Patti
Hope yo are "sitting pretty" in your new home. Health, Happiness & good fortune! To <u>you</u> always.
Any new large size pics? Signed in your usual wonderful fashion.
Your Ardent Admirer
Tony Skau
4044 Hampton Street
Elmhurst, L.I. NYC

Hi ! Patti
Hope the sketch pleases you?
Long time no hear. Any new pics?
How is the world treating you?
Your Artist Admirer
Henry Tony Skau
4044 Hampton Street
Elmhurst, L.I. NYC

Hi!
yes I love to sketch "sexy" and exciting you!!
Guess you have quite a collection by now.
All the pics you sent me are very exciting & nice. I go for them immensely. A wonderful group of unusual poses. Terrifically done. Mmmmmm!
Your Artist Admirer
Tony

Love
Kisses
Exciting
To- Patti
'61
HAG Jr.

Love
Kisses
Tony
"Patti"
'61'

The Nudes

Unless absolutely necessary for work, Patti Waggin was not inclined to appear nude in photos. Included here are two of Patti's rare nude shots, adjusted to keep within the bounds of the law. One is a well-known publicity shot. The other is a photo of Patti at sixteen, a newly wed married to Doug Craig, that has never been published before. Patti's marriage to Doug was short-lived, annulled by her mother when Doug wanted out. Doug was not thrilled with Patti's intended career choice. Despite his misgivings, during their brief marriage, Craig took four nude photos of Patti at her request, capturing images of her youthful, hope-filled, passionate self, which Doug Craig preserved throughout the decades.

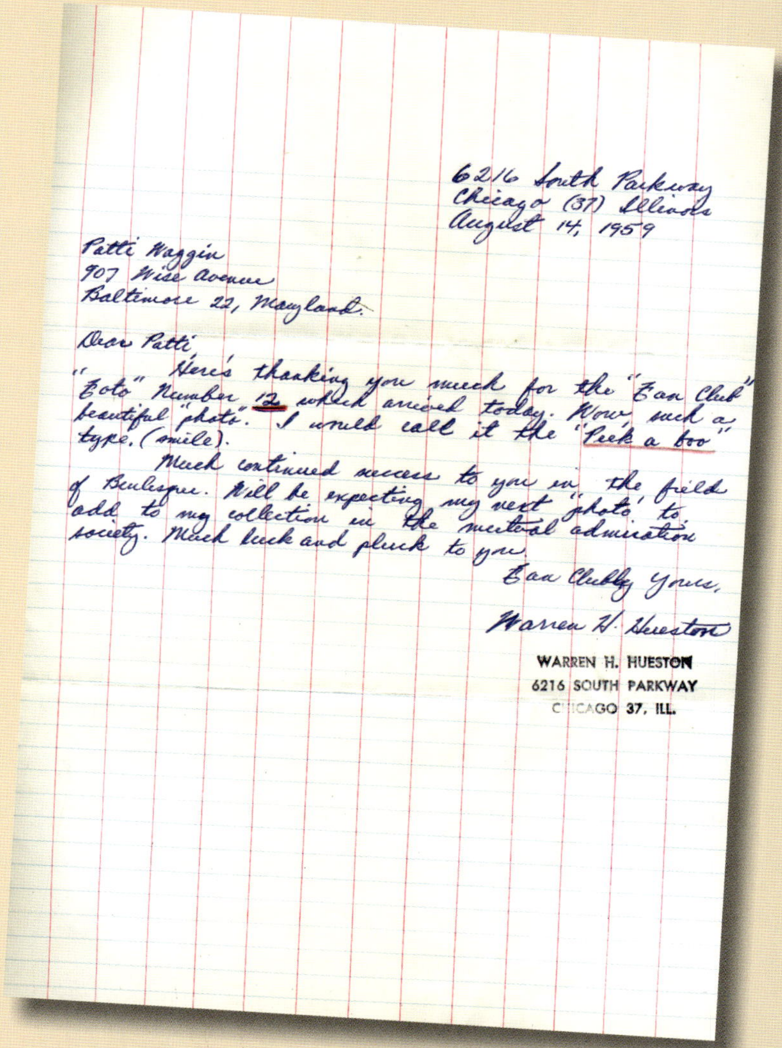

6216 South Parkway
Chicago (37) Illinois
August 14, 1959

Patti Waggin
907 Wise Avenue
Baltimore 22, Maryland.

Dear Patti,

Here's thanking you much for the "Fan Club" "Foto" Number 12 which arrived today. Wow, such a beautiful "photo". I would call it the "Peek a boo" type. (smile).

Much continued success to you in the field of Burlesque. Will be expecting my next "photo" to add to my collection in the mutual admiration society. Much luck and pluck to you.

Fan Clubly Yours,

Warren H. Hueston

WARREN H. HUESTON
6216 SOUTH PARKWAY
CHICAGO 37, ILL.

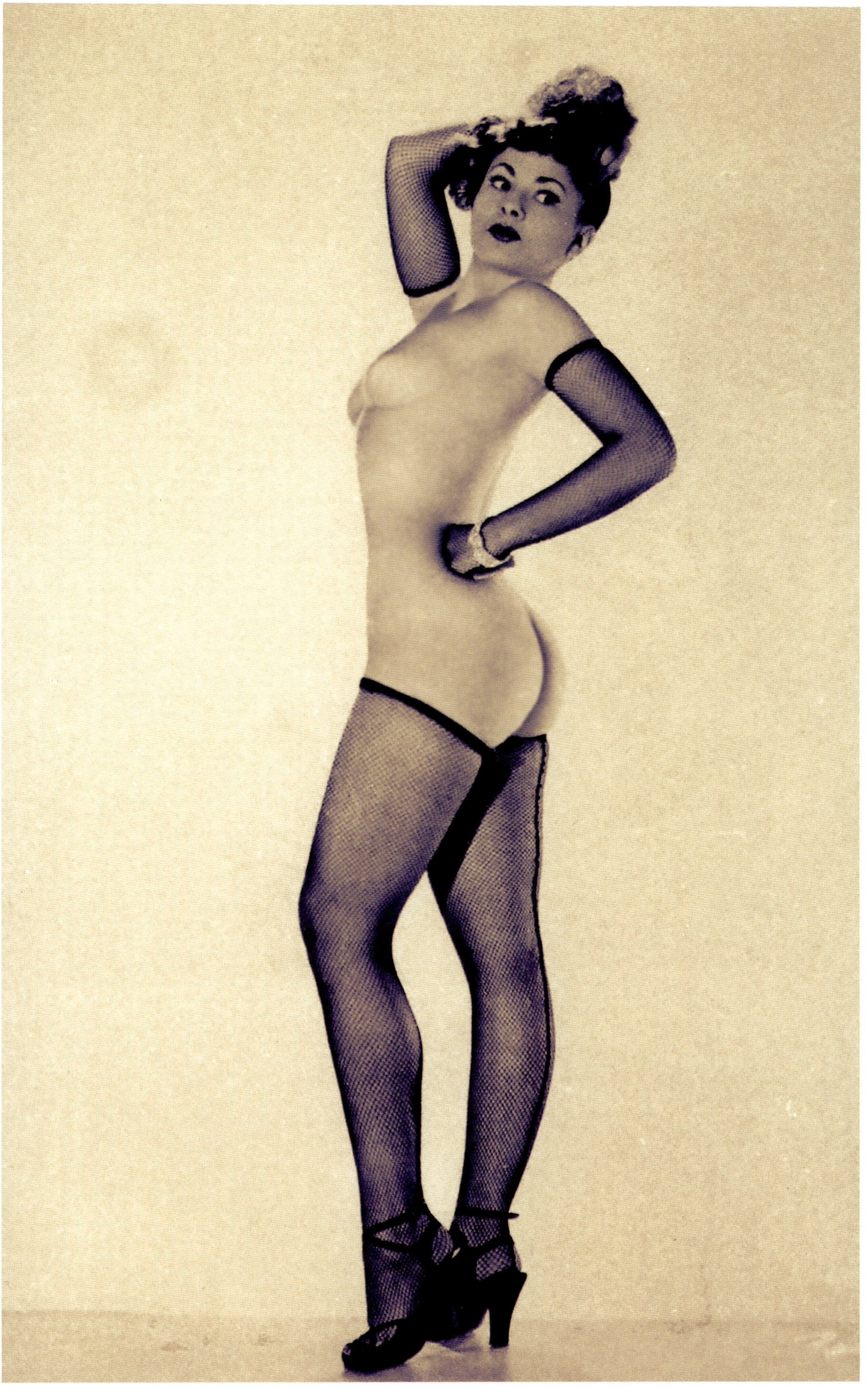

Nov. 4th, 1953

Ma Cher La Belle Bebe Patti:

I am at a loss for words to account for your failure to honor your appointment with me, and especially so because you proved to naieve to sift rumor from fact. The fact is that I am NOT married and haven't been married and for many years past, despite misconceptions and publicized rumors. Seems that if I am seen more than once with the same companion, the columnists have me "married." The one who is reputed now to be my "wife" is an employee, who would like to be Mrs. L.S. However, it is strictly a business relationship as far as it stands with me. My disappointment was equal to yours as I had planned a gala time together with you after such a long wait since we enjoyed a wonderful time.

If you will allow me, may I feel a little proud that you think so highly of me. I never suspected that your evident fondness for me was anything more than casual. Were it not for the fact that you were always involved in some personal affair, I might have made my adoration for you more evident. My feelings for you on this account had to be governed by the conventional respect and esteem that your attachment for another person merited.

Whenever you are again in your home town and can overlook this unfortunate misunderstanding, it will be my greatest pleasure to extend the most of cordial and affectionate greetings and have even better times together than we have missed..

Meanwhile, write as often as you can and whatever I can do for you professionally or otherwise, will be my privilege and pleasure. Keep me posted on your professional progress and send me a personally autographed photo. Al took your nudes away and I never saw them after that. Also include one for henpecked and plucked Pee J. It would be especially nice of you to remember him as he is the most abused man I know. (His daily allowance is 25-cents.)

Well, nuff sed. I will continue thinking of you as if nothing unpleasant occurred and will look forward to your occasional letters. Most affectionately and sincerely yours, (name signed unreadable)

P.S. We are now square. Merci Bien Et Beacu.

(Author's note: Mr. Looey Serbin of San Francisco addressed the letter to "Mlle. La Belle Patti Waggin, Danceuse Exotique Extraordinaire)

The Fans

Letters from Patti Waggin's fans ranged from the touchingly sweet to the entirely revolting with a little bit of desperate "please be mine" thrown in for good measure. Interestingly, several letters were recovered that had been penned by teens. One such letter references a show in which Patti had thrown postcards of herself to teenaged boys in the audience. One wonders exactly what was considered underaged for one of Patti's shows back in the day. Several of the correspondents stated they were just graduating high school and had been big fans of Patti's for years. It makes one wonder just how many youngsters slipped past the doorman to take in Patti's act.

Years after her career ended, Patti Waggin continued to receive and respond to fan mail. While fans of strippers have been known to be loyal followers of their favorites, Patti's fans exceeded all expectations. One wonders if it was Patti's personal touch that kept them writing. She dutifully answered all her fan mail and kept track of the details of the letters she answered. So strong was the impact of her correspondence over the years that, after Patti's death, her daughter received a condolence letter signed from "a friend" rather than "a fan."

The photos included here help round out the picture for us. In these images Patti is often shown backstage greeting fans who have traveled far and wide to come see her performance. Some of the men Patti is pictured with were average Joes, others were friends and family or colleagues. At least two of the folks shown here were famous faces from Hollywood back in the day, Donald O'Connor and Forrest Tucker. Study the photos closely. You never know who you might find captured in the crowd around Patti.

Patti was known to be headstrong and placed keeping the customers happy, treating them like VIP's, way ahead of adhering to management's rules. In one memorable image, Patti and a fan were captured standing right beside a sign reading "No Visitors Backstage."

PLACE
PIGALLE

551
ADMISSION
50¢
ADULTS ONLY
NO
PASSES
IN or
OUT
OPEN ALL NITE
TEASING
SIZZLING
TANTALIZING
The Inimitable
PATTI WAGGIN
in A PARISIAN PICKUP
TOO HOT
TO
HANDLE
HOME
OF
HITS

TOM
LARNER
MASTER
PROPS.

Niagara

Thursday 15

Patti

Well as of today I am a High School Grad. It sure is about time.

I'm sorry about me not writing. I really mean to write but I've been feeling pretty miserable lately.

The girl in the pictures and I have been dating pretty regularly. You told me to tell you when I got a girl friend. I guess she's her. Her name is Laurie White. Those pictures are of the night of our Senior Prom. Did you notice my tan.

My brother (Randy) is out there in Santa Monica. He's trying to make it on his own. My friend and I are going camping this week, and the next week I start work again.

My mother just got back from her vacation in Bermuda. Jimmy just back from Georgia. He was camping out also. I do miss you and I will see you in California in the near future.

How are you and everyone else? I miss you all.

Yours
Ralph
xoxoxoxoxo

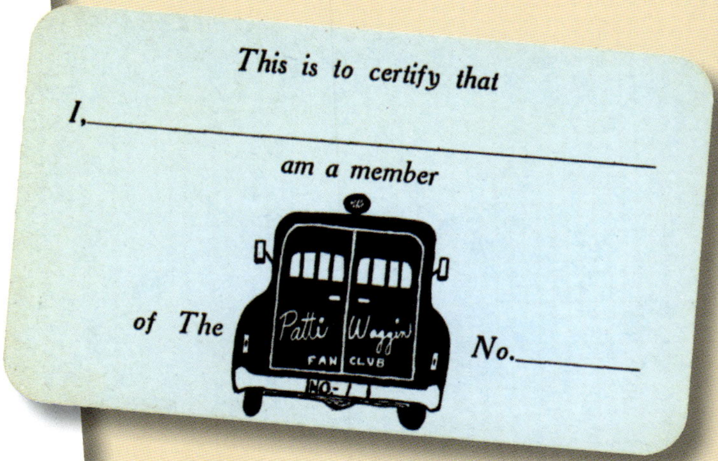

Las Vegas, Nevada
7/29/52

Pattie Dear

First of all please excuse paper and pencil but a friend of mine just returned from Lake Tahoe and said he saw your act while he was there. Nothing but compliments he said it was the best he had ever seen.

I sure hope you had better luck with you car going up there than you did from Frisco to here.

I went into L.A. last week but was only there for one day so didn't get around much. I just spent enough time to get a couple of Shuffle Alleys I wanted to catch your show but forgot where you said you were playing. Anyhow I don't think you had your engagement then.

It's funny I didn't catch at least one of your shows while you were here. But when you come back I will sit through all four of them. The weather here has really been on the hot side the last two weeks.

We have had some rain but it just makes it worse the humidity has really been high.

Right now "Vel Chessy" is in her third week, a new girl came in last night "Deborah Dean" "Little Miss Dream Girl" pretty too. Know her? Oh Irene Ryan was with Vel Chessy the first two weeks.

You haven't had any mail to come here how come? As sweet as you are you should have a continuous flow of mail.

Well dear enough for now. Again please excuse the paper and pencil but is all I have here at work. If you can find a few minutes to drop a line or two I would love it. Also want you to tell me where your at this next time I am in L.A. I can catch your show.

Truly Yours
Richard Decker "Day Bartender"
Embassy Club
1805 No. Main St. Las Vegas, Nev

Patti Can You Spare a Dime?

As you will see from the following letters, these fans were in a class all their own. They were looking for far more from their favorite stripper than a little correspondence and a few photos, and they were not afraid to ask.

Among the more demanding correspondents were: the aspiring actor who wanted Patti to connect him with the Hollywood crowd—after all, she lived close to Tinseltown and she had been an entertainer for many years; the musician offering her his original tunes; the baseball fan seeking an autographed ball from Don through Patti; the PhD studying strip clubs for his dissertation who wanted to visit Patti and other strippers in their various venues; the movie buff who wanted 8 MM film footage of Patti; and the fetishistic fan who wanted underwear Patti had worn in her act.

However, among the boldest of the lot were the man who asked for Patti's home phone number and the fellow who guardedly, slyly wrote that if Patti needed something "of a different nature" she should feel free to "call on me."

From the notes Patti made for herself on some of these letters and their envelopes, it is obvious Patti had a single concern related to these correspondents and their peculiar or lewd demands. She concerned herself with exactly how she would say no.

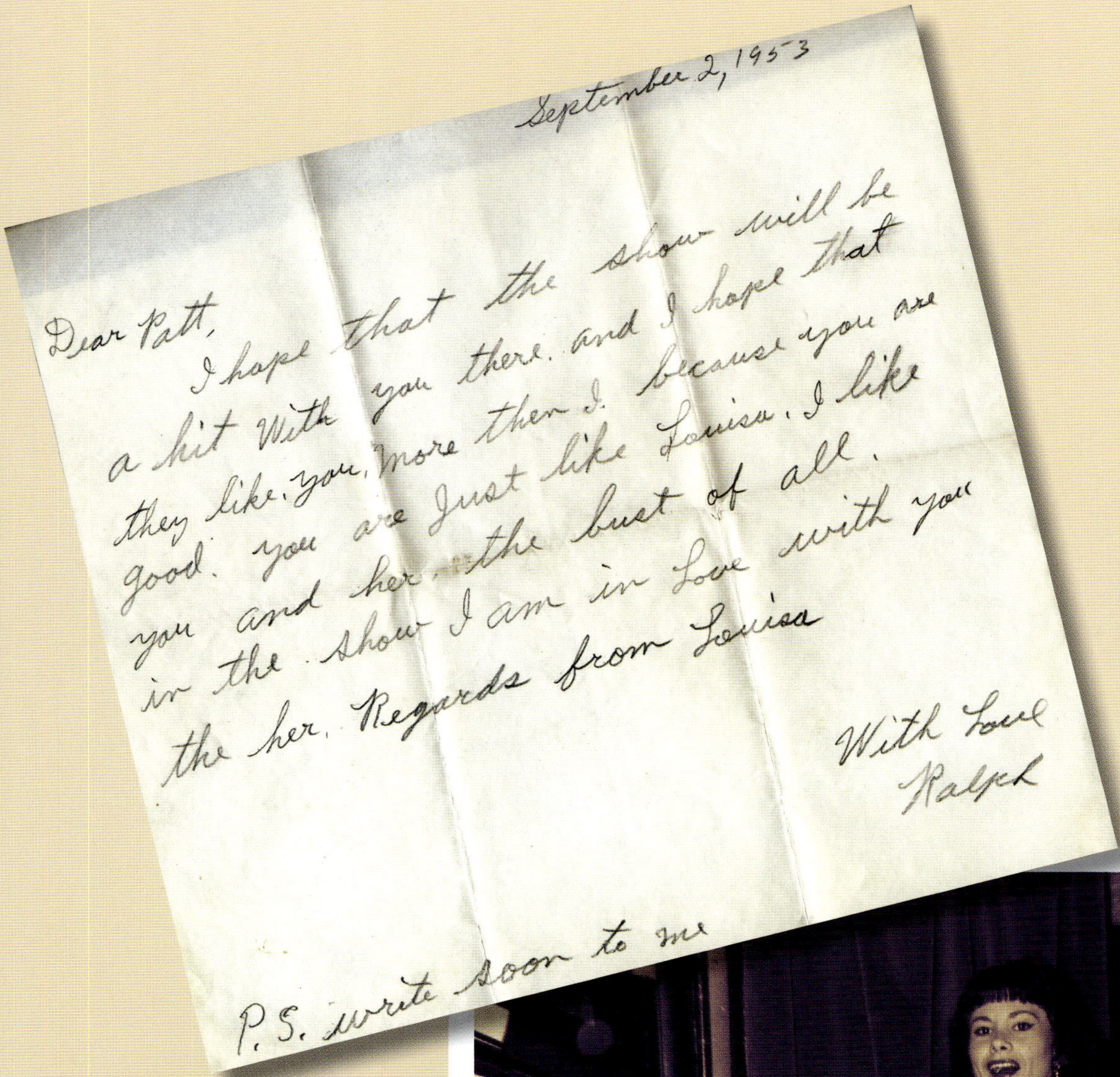

September 2, 1953

Dear Patt,

I hope that the show will be a hit With you there. and I hope that they like you, more then I. because you are good. you are Just like Louisa. I like you and her the bust of all in the Show I am in Love with you the her. Regards from Louisa

With Love
Ralph

P.S. write soon to me

PALACE
CONTINUOUS
BURLESK
PALACE
CONTINUOUS
BURLESK
Appearance in Buffalo!
MENS WEAR
Everything
DRASTICALLY
REDUCED
CONTINUOUS SHOWS
FORCED
TO
SELL
PATTI WAGGIN

EXIT

BOB WENZEL
858 N. MANSFIELD AVE.
HOLLYWOOD 38, CALIF.

MISS PATTI WAGGIN
907 WISE AVE.
BALTIMORE 22, MD.

DEAR PATTI:

FINALLY GOT AROUND TO JOINING YOUR FAN CLUB & AM LOOKING FORWARD TO RECEIVING YOUR PHOTO. HAVE ALWAYS BEEN A FAN OF YOURS SINCE 1955 WHEN YOU WORKED AT THE FOLLIES EVERY WEEK. SURE MISSYOU & WISH YOU COULD GET TO L.A. MORE THAN ONCE A YEAR. REALIZE OF COURSE THAT YOU WANT TO BE WITH YOUR HUSBAND DURING THE WINTER. HOPE HE HAS A GREAT BASEBALL SEASON IN 1961 & STRIKES OUT THE SIDE EVERY INNING.

SAW YOUR PERFORMANCE ON APRIL 3rd, 1960. CAUGHT ONE OF THE SMALL PHOTOGRAPHS YOU TOSS TO THE BOYS.

I HAD THE OPPORTUNITY (THE YEAR BEFORE) TO TALK TO YOU ON THE SIDEWALK AFTER THE LAST PERFORMANCE THE NIGHT THE TEENAGE BOYS IN THE AUDIENCE WENT A LITTLE BESERK (WHILE YOU WERE TOSSING OUT THE PHOTOS). I WAS AFRAID YOU MIGHT HAVE BEEN UPSET ABOUT IT, BUT YOU SAID YOU GOT A BIG KICK OUT OF IT. POSSIBLY YOU REMEMBER TALKING TO ME--THE FAT & 40 GUY ON THE SIDEWALK.

THINK YOU ARE A VERY LOVELY GIRL & WOW, WHAT A FIGURE!!

ALL THE BEST & COME TO L.A. AGAIN SOON.

Bob Wenzel

ome of
Enric
BREA

May 11, 1961

Dear Patti

I guess by this time you must be back in Sunny? California. How was your trip? I know the people of So. America must have been crazy about you. I don't see how they could help it. Anyway, I'm glad you are back.

Are you appearing someplace around here now? I would sure like to see you again. I really think you are one of the most desirable women I have ever seen. As I once said, I'm sorry you are married because to be with you for one evening would be a great thrill for me. Couldn't you lose your hubby for one evening and let me take you out for dinner and dancing? Please don't think I'm being bold because I know you couldn't do it, but I can dream can't I?

How about letting me know where you are appearing so I can come over some evening. Also I hope you haven't forgotten that I have a picture coming. Can hardly wait to get it.

More later, Bye for now.
Love Roger (over)

Roger Wilson
3053 La Corona Ave.
Altadena, Calif.
Sy.4-6317

See I am being bold. Throwing in my phone number. Shame on me! Do you ever talk to your fans in person or by phone? Or is it just wishful thinking again?
Bye, Roger

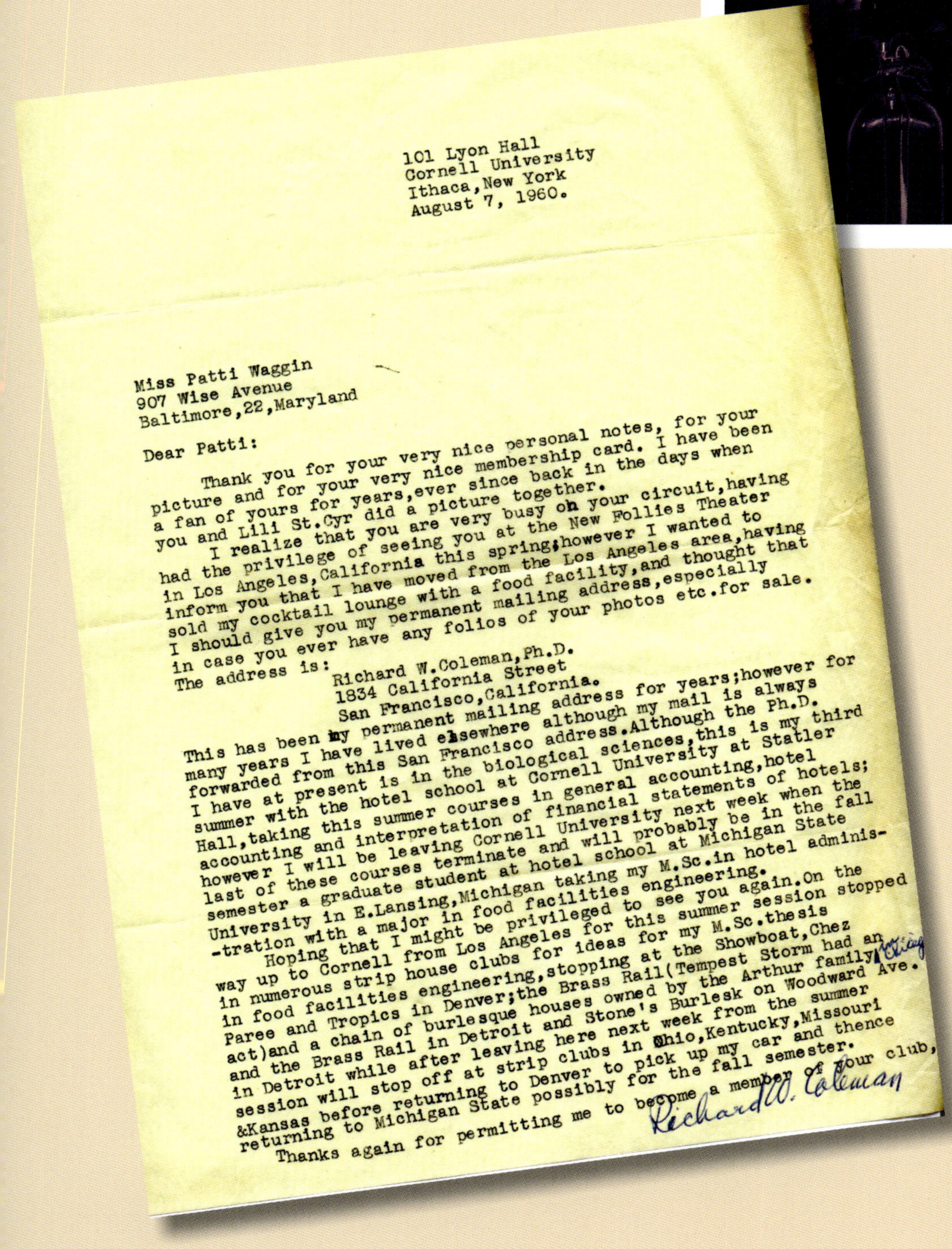

101 Lyon Hall
Cornell University
Ithaca,New York
August 7, 1960.

Miss Patti Waggin
907 Wise Avenue
Baltimore,22,Maryland

Dear Patti:

Thank you for your very nice personal notes, for your picture and for your very nice membership card. I have been a fan of yours for years,ever since back in the days when you and Lili St.Cyr did a picture together.

I realize that you are very busy on your circuit,having had the privilege of seeing you at the New Follies Theater in Los Angeles,California this spring;however I wanted to inform you that I have moved from the Los Angeles area,having sold my cocktail lounge with a food facility,and thought that I should give you my permanent mailing address,especially in case you ever have any folios of your photos etc.for sale. The address is:

Richard W.Coleman,Ph.D.
1834 California Street
San Francisco,California.

This has been my permanent mailing address for years;however for many years I have lived elsewhere although my mail is always forwarded from this San Francisco address.Although the Ph.D. I have at present is in the biological sciences,this is my third summer with the hotel school at Cornell University at Statler Hall,taking this summer courses in general accounting,hotel accounting and interpretation of financial statements of hotels; however I will be leaving Cornell University next week when the last of these courses terminate and will probably be in the fall semester a graduate student at hotel school at Michigan State University in E.Lansing,Michigan taking my M.Sc.in hotel adminis-tration with a major in food facilities engineering.

Hoping that I might be privileged to see you again.On the way up to Cornell from Los Angeles for this summer session stopped in numerous strip house clubs for ideas for my M.Sc.thesis in food facilities engineering,stopping at the Showboat,Chez Paree and Tropics in Denver;the Brass Rail(Tempest Storm had an act)and a chain of burlesque houses owned by the Arthur family in Chicago and the Brass Rail in Detroit and Stone's Burlesk on Woodward Ave. in Detroit while after leaving here next week from the summer session will stop off at strip clubs in Ohio,Kentucky,Missouri &Kansas before returning to Denver to pick up my car and thence returning to Michigan State possibly for the fall semester.

Thanks again for permitting me to become a member of your club,

Richard W. Coleman

MORE & MORE
JACKPOTS
SILVER
SLIPPER
GAMBLING HALL
HAPPY DAZE REVUE
JIMMY SHAW
PATTI WAGGIN
HANK HENRY KULDIP SINGH
DANCING
RESTAURANT
BAR
OPEN 24 HOURS

PIGALLE
WAGGIN

1409 E. 23rd Street
Winston–Salem, N.C.
Feb. 8, 1955
Lillian Hunt
New Follies
Los Angeles, Calif.

Dear Madam:

Some time ago, it was my good fortune to see Miss Patti Waggin perform one of the most delightful acts that it has been my priviledge to see. I am writing this letter to obtain information as to her bookings, so that I might arrange to see her act again. I do not know if this information is available to me or not, however, if you can tell me her bookings for June, July or August, I certainly would like to have this information.

Are there any pictures of her that may be obtained? I would like to have some very much as she is one of the most beautiful women that I have ever seen.

Please find enclosed a stamped self addressed envelope for your convienence in answering my letter; that is if you choose to do so.

This letter is not the raving of a lunatic, but a frantic request for information. I got your name and address from <u>Billboard</u>.

Thanking you for all information you can give me on the beautiful Miss Patti Waggin, I remain.

Sincerely
Al Thomas

THE CO ED
WITH THE EDUCATED
TORSO
Patti
WAGGIN
no
COVER
no
ADMISSION
America's Most
Gorgeous and
Youthful
UNDRAPED DANCING
STAR

The Inimitable
PATTI WAGGIN
in A PARISIAN PICKUP
TOO HOT
TO
HANDLE
OPEN ALL NITE
TEASING
SIZZLING
TANTALIZING
The Inimitable
PATTI WAGGIN
in A PARISIAN PICKUP
TOO HOT
TO
HANDLE

John Sweeny
Miller Hall
Mount Union College
Alliance, Ohio

Dear Miss Waggin,

I saw your show in Pittsburgh about a year ago and enjoyed it, to say the least. There were two things that impressed me greatly about you. I am, in this letter, seeking an 8x10 reminder of your more than worthy attributes, namely, a picture. I expect no more than your other fans and probably desire no less. I claim to be no connoiseur of the art of disrobing, on the stage, at any rate. I would be proud to be a member of your fan club and will promote you whenever possible. If you ever need assistance of a different nature please feel free to call upon me. I hope that pictures are still available, if not, I would be more than happy to take my own. I close this letter in hopes that you will be coming to a near-by theater and that there are no longer any pictures available.

Respectfully yours,

John Sweeny

John Sweeny

BOXES
1.75
NO PERSONS UNDER 18 PERMITTED

The World
owes you a living
but you have to work
hard to collect it.

Hi Patti darling,

How have you been I hoped you well and happy. I have been thinking of you and know you wonder why I haven't wrote. But honey I figure you get so many letters concerning your fan club that maybe you just don't care but I do think you are very sweet a little china doll. And hope to see your act again real soon as I know it is very clever with such a sweet girl. I love all the wonderful pictures you send me these so cute and sweet and honey I do want another photo of you to look at and hold when I start thinking of you. I do wish I knew you personally and could say yes I know you as a personal friend in my business I come in contact with many show girls models and have many personal friends among them I do wish I could meet you and add you to the list

As I have said before and I know it to be true as any agents tell me so. You and I have many things in common one of the reasons for your forming your fan club and advertising in Indianapolis, Ind for members to form your Club. Yes Patti darling I do know your season better than you think and honey I love you for it more than words will ever say.

And I never can get to many photos of a little darling such as you. So please forgive me for not writing sooner and I will be looking for a picture of you sweetheart real soon. I am giving you my Indianapolis box number as I would like you to send it to this box as it makes me so proud to receive a photo of you when I go to pick up my mail that I love to carry it all the way from Indianapolis to Fort Wayne.

Well Patti I guess I had better close for now and maybe I might send you a nice gift of lingerie such as pattie and bra the kind a fellow likes to look and the kind that reveals your mose personal self forgive me Patti dear but it would be a very great thrill to see you model in pattis and bra the patties the kind that reveal inimate things.

Well bye now sweetheart and do think of me once in a while as I do of you my little china doll all my love goes out to you baby and I will be waiting to hear and receive your cute photo real soon. Bye now.

Love & Kisses
Your friend

Johnny

Honey I am giving you my address as I know you might get confused as you receive so many letters so here it is

John Brisboe
Post Office Box 685
Indianapolis, Indiana

Send it to Indianapolis instead of my box at Fort Wayne will you please sweetheart I will love you for it.

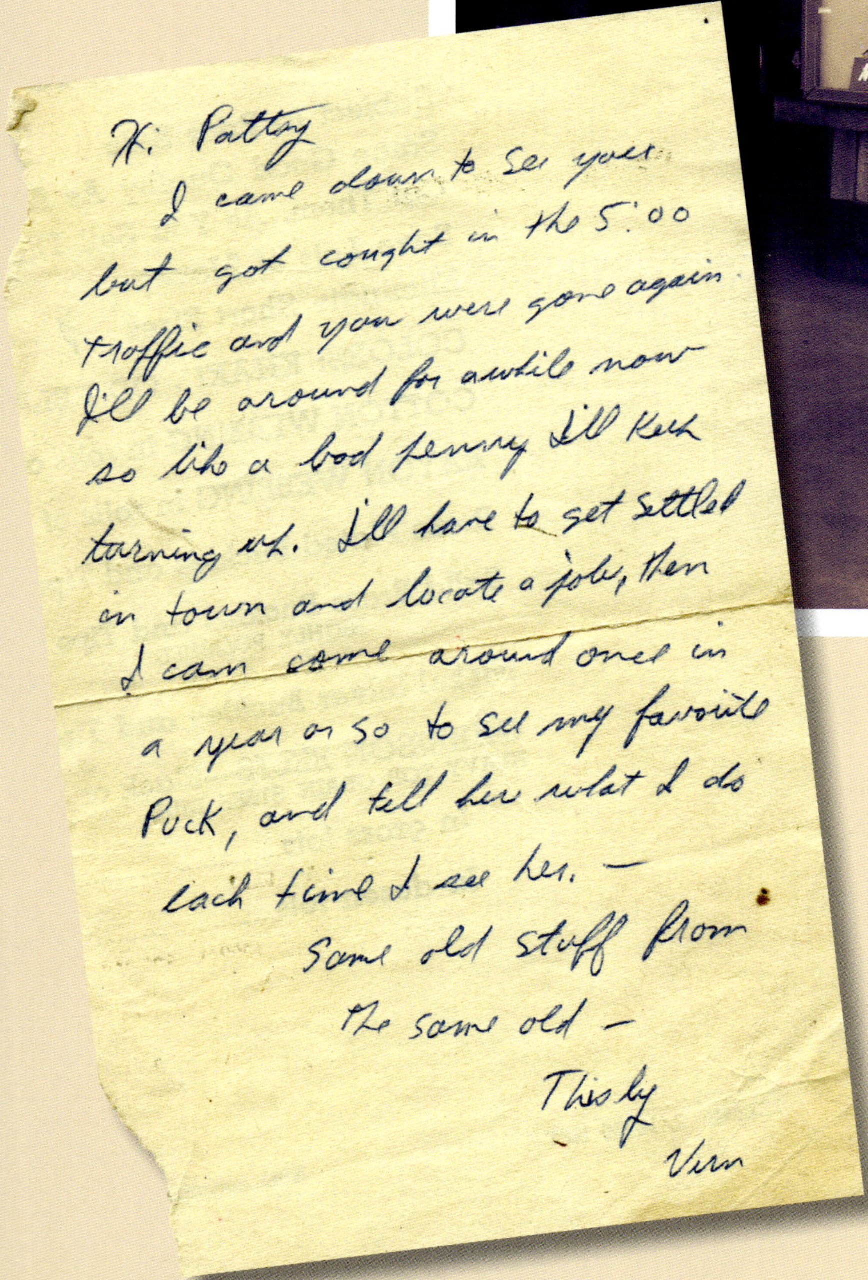

Hi Patty
I came down to see you
but got caught in the 5:00
traffic and you were gone again
I'll be around for awhile now
so like a bad penny I'll keep
turning up. I'll have to get settled
in town and locate a job, then
I can come around once in
a year or so to see my favorite
Puck, and tell her what I do
each time I see her. —
Same old stuff from
the same old —
Thisly
Vern

Christmas 1960
Miss Patti Waggin
907 Wise Avenue
Baltimore 22, Md

Dearest Patti Darlin'

Well Honey I have been somewhat lax in your Darlingest of fan Clubs, since becoming a member of same, But Ken. Will just have to get on the ball and send for some more of little Petite Patti's Phan Club Photos, Won't I honey? – and another thing Patti Darlin' I never did write and thank you for those cute panties, and stage hose you sent to yours truly so I herewith take this means of doing so My Darling. I really really appreciated your sending them too me, and thanks a thousand my Honey Doll Patti for those things. Now I have been rather busy for some time now honey Doll but I always try to think of and to send Greetings to my friends and Sweet little cuddling cuties like you at Christmas time so therefore Patti honey, please give me an answer to this letter soon as you can Honey or at your convenience.

And I shall appreciate it to the utmost coming from you Patti honey. Now I have a few questions which I would like for you to ans. For me, honey. When you do write too me, some of the questions I asked you before but you never answered for me honey.

1. you never did tell me if you and Don Rudolph, the baseball pitcher are still man and wife and are still married. I understand that Don is now property of our Indianapolis Indians right here in Indiana. And still another question. Are you currently playing on the Burlesk stage I have been to the Fox in Indianapolis several times lately but have never seen you, nor any of the best performers, or Burlesque Queens on the Fox Stage. So what is going on in the Burlesk Circuit honey? Please put me wise baby tell me sumpin – or Sumpin – I don't care to see the Worst performers. I want to see the best and Patti baby I consider you the Be-e-e-st (the very very best believe me baby doll)

So Patti Please let Ken know what gives and what goes, ha.

and one more question Doll. You never told me your age honey and I've asked you that one several times so won't you please tell Ken your age Honey bun? Please.

Wishing you the merriest of Christmases and a happy holiday with dreams of love.

Kenneth

You mentioned about the 8MM film of you doing a semi-strip. What do you ask for the film on this Honey? Please Know I haven't any such camera now though. Is Patti Waggin your stage name or real name. If it's your stage name What is your real name Honey? Will try and order lots of your Roses this coming year.

Love. Ken.
Kenneth E. Friend
513 North Carver Street
Greensburg, Indiana
phone 3-6062

Lighter Moments

Life for a Burlesque Queen wasn't all hard work and fan mail. In between the shows and the contrived glamour of it all, there was time for fun and for a life to be lived. In time, Patti progressed from a young sex-kitten of the stage to the wife of a big league ballplayer. Every step along the way had its moments.

The late 1940s brought Patti as close to earthly paradise as one could get when she joined the aforementioned six girl dance troupe, the Hollywood Debs. The Debs sailed from San Francisco to the island paradise of Honolulu, Hawaii, and a tour of the best clubs the island had to offer.

This was Patti's first trip abroad, Hawaii was not yet a state, and, based on her own photo album, she made the most of it. Photos of Patti vary from beach lounging to racing around the island on a motorcycle, either rented or borrowed from one of the guys. Her passion for motorcycles would keep her on two wheels well into her sixties.

Patti's agent, Lillian Hunt (who would later produce a few low budget burlesque films), watched over her girls like a mother hen and threw in some practical advice amidst the fun. In one letter, Hunt admonished Patti to study the contract she was to sign and made very clear what sort of accommodations Patti should expect to have. Hunt ended the letter with, "Make sure they spell your name right." These were words to the wise from someone who knew. As you can clearly see in the accompanying photo, here's at least one marquee that got her name wrong. Patti's first name is missing a "t" and her last name an "l". Fellow "It Girl" Mitzi Dore's first name is missing the final "i" as well.

Stage hands were good for "surprise" cakes on birthdays. Bare Magazine captured one birthday celebration for Patti in their February 1954 edition. The article declared that Patti had recently celebrated her twenty-first birthday. Considering Patti was born in 1926, they were only a few years off. No matter, facts were nothing. Bare was interested in the photos they took of Patti receiving a "birthday spanking" from her fellow burlesque queens and the shot of the Sex Oomph Girl showing off her flexibility as she straddled her candle festooned double layer birthday cake. The whole affair took place at the El Rey Theater in Oakland, California.

Finally, as the wife of a ball player working hard to impress the big brass, Patti accompanied Don on his trips playing Winter Ball in Venezuela and Cuba. Heading to the tropical climes of Latin America held many opportunities for fun in the Winter League towns ... provided you dodged the occasional hail of bullets. At this point Cuba was still friendly to Americans and baseball was flourishing in the tropics. Perhaps there were also a few motorcycles that needed to be ridden.

Patti Waggin

(THE CO-ED WITH THE EDUCATED TORSO)

ATWATER 4-4859

907 WISE AVE.
BALTIMORE 22, MD.

PHONE MADISON 9-1868

2

LILLIAN HUNT
ANNA EVA BIGGS

Winsor-Hunt Theatrical Agency

337½ SOUTH MAIN STREET
LOS ANGELES 13, CALIF.

Now Patti be sure that is all in there before you sign. Also 6 days weekly you close in Las Vegas the 3rd of Jan. They want you to open in Colorado Springs the 4th of Jan. Find out if you can fly in there from Vegas and make it for the 4th. Nothing new since I wrote you. Anxious to see you. Venus is still sick. Guess she will get back about the same time you do. Let me hear from you at once regarding Colorado Springs. Take care of yourself. Everyone says hello.

Love.

Lillian

Be sure they spell your name right

BURLESQUE
NEW LIBERTY
33 SOUTH CENTER
Telephone 5-3113
ALL NEW SHOW
with NEW SUMMER PRICES
MATINEE—All Seats 60c
EVENINGS—General Admission..... 60c
RESERVED—First Ten Rows.......$1.20
The greatest NAME and Headliner in Burlesque Today!
PATTIE
"BROWNELL"
She's Here! In Person in the Most Sexsational Dance Ever Attempted Anywhere.
EXTRA — Also in Person — EXTRA
VIRGINIA BEACH
The Girl Who Strips to Please!
Burlesque's Newest UNCOVER GIRL
PLUS
A Great Array of Burlesque Stars With
BILLY COLLINS
and a Hilarious Comedy
20 — CAST OF — 20
THE LIBERTY TEASETTES
"TEN OF THE CUTEST LITTLE NUDISTS"
DOORS OPEN DAILY 1 P.M.
BARGAIN MATINEES DAILY
ALL SEATS 60c
3 STAGE SHOWS TODAY
LATE SHOW TONIGHT
Midnite Show Every Sat. Night
LADIES FREE!
Make Up a Party! Bring the Ladies! They'll Howl!

S.S. MATSONIA
SAN FRANCISCO
S.S. MATSONIA
SAN FRANCISCO

Keith Bernard

Don't Take It So Personally!

Robert De Niro's film The Fan depicts the dark side of fan devotion. There are times when some fans do not understand or respect the boundaries and try to get far too close to the person they adore. In the world of strippers, this could be dangerous. While most strippers, including Patti, lived professional lives free of violent incidents, others were not so lucky. Given that Patti gave out both her Baltimore and Los Angeles home addresses to the members of her Patti Waggin Fan Club for correspondence, things could have gone much differently.

Captured here are a few of the letters from fans who were becoming much too attached to Patti for comfort. One young man states he broke up with his high school girlfriend as he can't stop thinking about Patti. Another man, thwarted by Patti in some request no doubt, declares this to be his last letter, despite his protestations of his unflagging love for her. A third does his best to impress Patti, describing himself and his oil wells. Then again, he makes no mention of whether or not those wells are producing. One doubts this is a lonely T. Boone Pickens or Sultan eager to lavish his fortune upon the ever-popular Patti Waggin.

Los Angeles 18 Calif.

Hello Patti darling

I was talking to Nola and she said she received a letter from you listen Patti darling if I ever hurt you I am very sorry Patti darling. I love you very much. I take my daughter and myself and leave New York head for England, Norway, Sweden, Denmark, France and Germany. Then back to the United States.

Please Patti darling answer my letter and let me no when you will be in Los Angeles Calif and which shows you will be at Patti Waggin Darling I love you more than you will ever no. I belong to the Latter Day Saints or they call us Morm's But all I want to see is you Patti Waggin darling And please answer my letter All my love is for you Patti Waggin darling

XXXXXXXXXXXXXXXXX

Please answer my letter

Yours Respectfully

Joseph Jacobsen

1782 West 24 Street

Los Angeles 18 Calif

Los Angeles 18 Calif.

My Darling Patti Waggin

this is my last letter to you. I was talking to Nola that work for Sug Welsh she said she received a letter from you. Well I guess you put me in the dog house. Patti I am only 63 years old. But I love you very much. I ask you if you would please send me a picture of me and my house I gave you as I will leave today for Japan.

May not see you for a while Please Patti darling send me that picture also let me no when you will be in Los Angeles Calif. Patti Waggin darling I love you more than you will ever no xxxxooxxxxxx

Hope to see you this year darling so will close

Lots of Love

Joseph Jacobsen

1782 West 24 Street

Los Angeles 18 Calif

Answer my letter soon honey.

Dear Patti,

Your recent letter to me made me very happy indeed. There is one thing I've come to treasure and that is your beautiful friendship. When I did not hear from you over the Holidays and also when my small gift was returned to me by the post master as unclaimed I presumed our beautiful friendship had come to an end. I feel very badly I couldn't understand why. So I gave your gift to one of my sisters and tried to figure why you returned the Christmas gift. However your letter has cleared that all up and I feel quite happy about it all. I didn't realize you were in South America. In the meantime I will try to make up for the Xmas gift in my small way.

Good luck on your new home. I hear that San Fernando Valley is a beautiful place to live. I hope you two wonderful people will have all the happiness in the world.

One thing I've come to treasure your friendship through these many years and I mean to keep it as long as I'm alive because you have personified on stage the "beautiful woman" to an artist eyes and I've seen many beautiful women in my work, but not many can compare to you.

As you may know I live with my mother. In her late years we decided to do our inside house over again. I have a brother-in-law who is quite an artist in the construction field and what a beautiful job he has done for "mom" who spends quite a few hours in the kitchen.

I will have some color photos taken of myself in the kitchen and you will see the beauty in "Pink and pearl gray" colors –Where "mom" will spend the remaining years of her life surrounded by beauty.

Love Vincent

PEN
ALL
IGHT
PICTURES THAT
ARE DIFFERENT
HOTE
SENSATIONAL HITS
The Inimitable
PATTI WAGGIN
in A PARISIAN PICKUP
TEASING
SIZZLING
TANTALIZING
TOO HOT
TO
HANDLE
ETIES

KLEENEX

174 BELMONT AVENUE
BELLEVILLE 7, N.J.
JUNE 19, 1961

DEAR PATTI :

I JUST READ YOUR LETTER AND AM VERY GLAD TO HEAR FROM YOU. I THOUGHT I WOULD NEVER HEAR FROM YOU AGAIN, SINCE I READ IN THE PAPER ABOUT YOUR GETTING MARRIED. I HOPE YOU WILL FORGIVE MY TYPING THIS LETTER BECAUSE I DON'T THINK YOU COULD UNDERSTAND MY HANDWRITING. EVEN THE RIBBON ON THIS MACHINE IS PRETTY WELL WORN.

I UNDERSTAND FROM YOUR LETTER YOU WERE ON TOUR IN SOUTH AMERICA. YOU MUST WRITE ME A NICE LONG LETTER TELLING ME ABOUT ALL THE INTERESTING PLACES YOU VISITED. AS FAR AS THE CHRISTMAS CARD I WILL ALWAYS REMEMBER AND BE THINKING OF YOU. I WILL BE GETTING MARRIED IN ABOUT A YEAR AND I HOPE YOU WILL OF COURSE HONOR ME WITH YOUR PRESENTS AT THE CHURCH AND RECEPTION. I WILL LET YOU KNOW BY SPECIAL INVITATION WHEN AND WHERE IT WILL BE.

THE PICTURE I HAVE OF YOU IS ABOUT 3 YEARS OLD, I IMAGINE YOU HAVE QUITE A FEW NEW ONES SINCE THE TIME YOU WERE IN NEWARK, N.J. THERE IS NO NUMBER ON THE PICTURE. IF POSSIBLE COULD YOU SEND ME A FEW DIFFERENT POSES BECAUSE I WOULD LIKE TO START A PHOTO COLLECTION ON YOU. IF THERE IS ANY CHARGE FOR THE PHOTOS PLEASE LET ME KNOW AND AS SOON AS I RECEIVE THEM I WILL SEND THE MONEY. ALSO WHEN YOU HAVE ANY TAKEN IN THE FUTURE WILL YOU PLEASE LET ME KNOW SO THAT I CAN KEEP MY COLLECTION UP TO DATE. EVERYONE HERE IS FINE AND WELL, HOPE YOU AND YOUR HUSBAND ARE WELL. CAN IMAGINE YOU ARE JUST AS BEAUTIFUL AS EVER///

I WAS VERY HAPPY TO HEAR THAT YOU BOUGHT A NEW HOME IN CALIFORNIA, COULD YOU SEND ME A SNAPSHOT OF IT. ALSO COULD YOU SEND ME A PHOME NUMBER WHERE I COULD CALL YOU SOMETIME AND SURPRISE YOU. I AM WRITING THIS AT WORK WILL HAVE TO CLOSE NOW. WILL WAIT ANXIOUSLY FOR YOUR LETTER AND PHOTOS. THANKS SO VERY MUCH FOR WRITING AND LETTING ME KNOW THAT YOU ARE WELL.

SO LONG FOR NOW::::

A TRUE FREIND ALWAYS

Pat Sisbarro

PAT SISBARRO

May 18, 1961.

Dear Patti,

As I haven't heard from you, no letter nor no picture, I wonder if you got back to Calif. all O.K. from your South American trip.

We had 8 34/100 inches rain from Thurs. to Tues. - rivers and creeks all out, and so many roads closed, so many people homeless, worst flood since 1937.

Sun is out nice and warm, so many flowers in bloom, Ind. looks nice now.

I had a virus, sick for several months, but feeling better now, it took a lot of my friends, guess I was just too tough.

Well Patti, Please write and Please send photo, revealing one, I can frame, and please write something nice on it.

Bye for now.

Sincerely,
Clarence Huxford
P.O. Box 391
Clinton, Ind.

P.S. How do you like living in Calif.?

513 North Carver St.
Greensburg, Indiana
July 10th, 1961
Miss Patti Waggin
15718 Index
Granada Hills, Calif.

Dear Honey Bun;

I really was so nice hearing from you again after such an elapse of time. I am behind on this letter I know since I rec'd yours on date of June, 12th last but please forgive me as I was away from home at time your letter arrived.

Was up in Canada fishing and hunging with some friends, had a Good time, but eat up with mosquitos, ha. Well Honey Bun so you are 27 yrs. of age, well to me you look 22 or 23 so looks are Deceiving, right? Ha.

I see where your husband Don's record with the Indians is now 9 and 5. Not bad at all. I never go see the Indians Play ball, since I'm all Major league, I go see the Cincy Reds Play a lot and naturally being so close to home, they are my team, and Frankie Robinson and Eddie Kasko are my favorite Players on Cincinnati Reds Club. I would sure like to see you in Person and sit down and have a long talk with you some time, honey bun, if that is or were Possible as I've said many times before. I will say again Patti Dear – you are above all the rest of the Burlesk Queens as far as I'm concerned and you are my Honey doll of all the Burlesk Circuit Patti Dear, so you got down to S.A. (meaning South America) I hope you liked it down there and enjoyed yourself while there baby.

Well now Patti Honey bun be sure and ans. This letter, honey real real soon and let me know about all I'm going to ask you about.

As I said before you are my favorite above all of them, and I do want some more of your Photos a little later on When I can find a Place to handle them and to put them but right now My Quarters are Kinda small and haven't the room to take care of more of your sweet Pictures, but you can bet I'll find room Darling Patti ha. Well now here are my questions I wish to ask you about ?????

Author's Note: That was how the letter ended.

Domino
SIERRA
Interpretive Dancer
RAVEENA
Queen of Pantomime
STARRING
PATTIE WAGGIN
THE CO-ED
WITH THE EDUCATED TORSO!
The TOKYE TRIO
DAVE TOWNSEND
Orchestra
FLOOR SHOWS
Nitely
TOWNSEND
Excellent
DINNERS

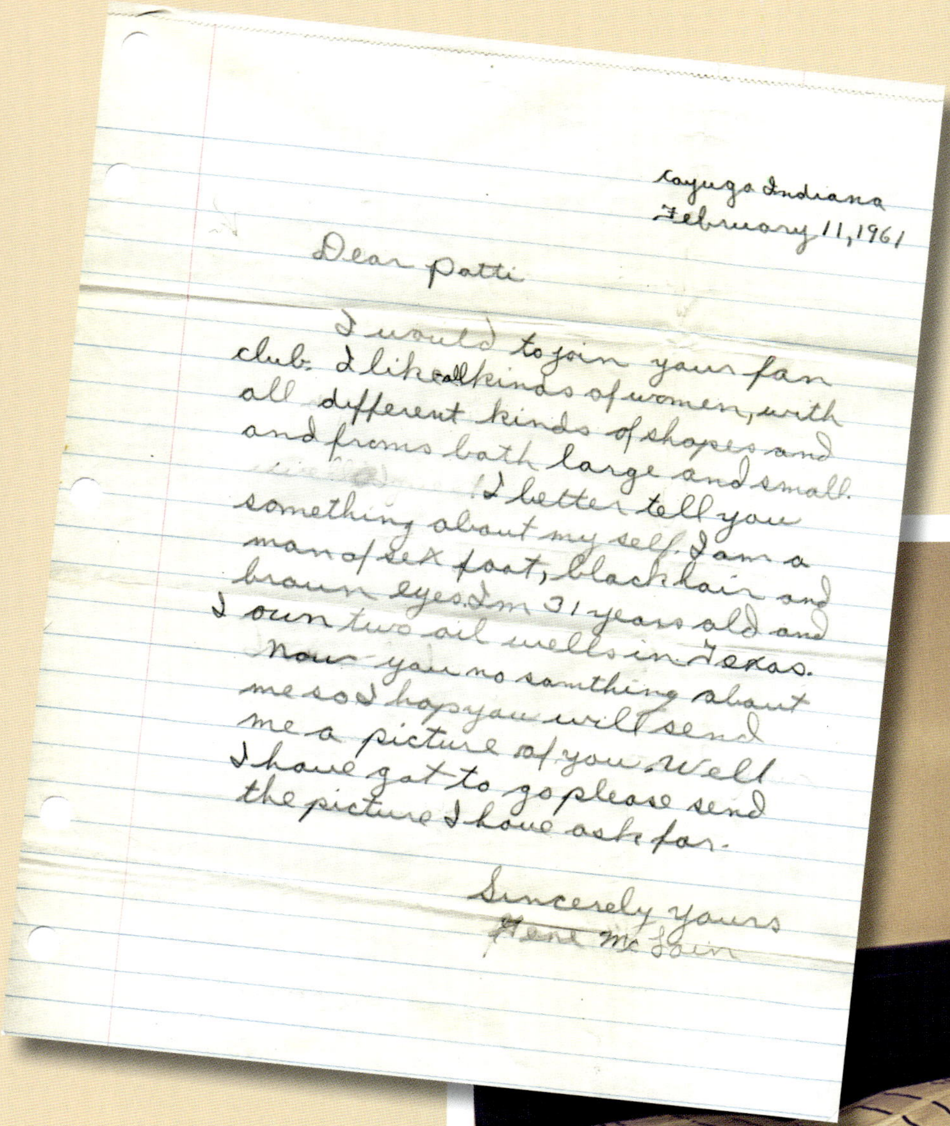

Cayuga Indiana
February 11, 1961

Dear Patti

I would to join your fan club. I like all kinds of women, with all different kinds of shapes and and froms both large and small.

I better tell you something about my self. I am a man of sex foot, black hair and brown eyes. I'm 31 years old and I own two oil wells in Texas.

Now you no samthing about me so I hope you will send me a picture of you. Well I have got to go please send the picture I have ask for.

Sincerely yours
Gene Mc Lain

Candid Patti in some more unique moments.

PHONE MAdison 9-1868

LILLIAN HUNT
ANNA EVA BIGGS

Winsor-Hunt Theatrical Agency

337½ SOUTH MAIN STREET
LOS ANGELES 13, CALIF.

Dear Patti

Got your note and a letter from Bob Corash which I am enclosing. I tried to get fare for you but as you can see in the letter he will not pay it. At first he said he wouldn't hire anyone for more than 2 weeks and 200.00 a week and I turned him down. Nothing less than 250.00 a week and 4 week contract so if it is alright with you go up and sign the contracts. Now be sure the contracts are worded right before you sign them. Like this

4 consecutive weeks. no option

$250.00 weekly

Artist agrees to pay Bob Corash Agency 5% Comm.

Artist shall receive sole headline billing in all advertising, lights, display, programs, 100% type.

Patti the athlete shows off her skills, which were unique to her act.

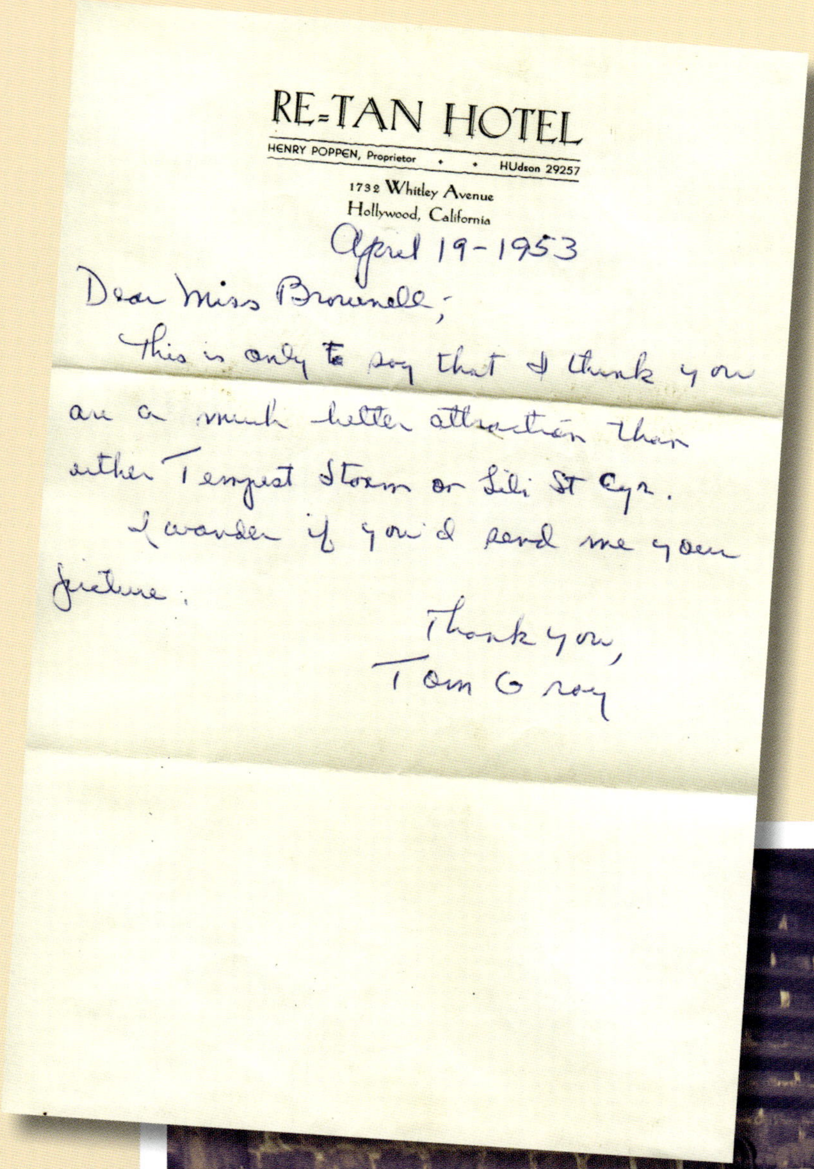

RE-TAN HOTEL

HENRY POPPEN, Proprietor • • HUdson 29257

1732 Whitley Avenue
Hollywood, California

April 19-1953

Dear Miss Brownell;

This is only to say that I think you are a much better attraction than either Tempest Storm or Lili St Cyr.

I wonder if you'd send me your picture.

Thank you,
Tom Gray

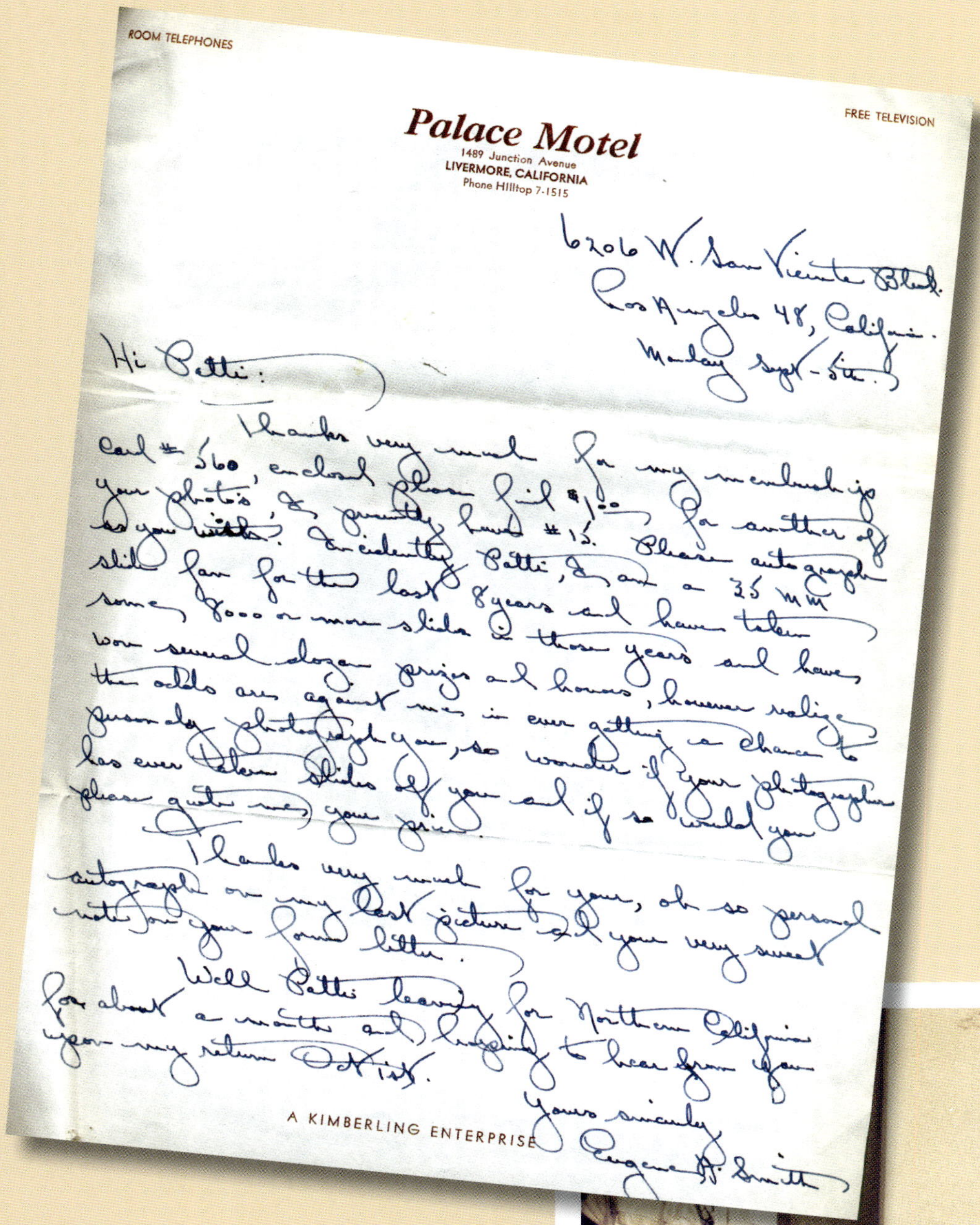

ROOM TELEPHONES

FREE TELEVISION

Palace Motel
1489 Junction Avenue
LIVERMORE, CALIFORNIA
Phone Hilltop 7-1515

6206 W. San Vicente Blvd.
Los Angeles 48, California.
Monday Sept - 5th.

Hi Patti:

Thanks very much for my membership card #560, enclosed please find $1.00 for another of your photo's, I presently have #15. Please autograph as you wish. Incidently Patti, I am a 35 MM slide fan for the last 8 years and have taken some 8000 or more slides in those years and have won several dozen prizes and honors, however realize the odds are against me in ever getting a chance to personaly photograph you, so wonder if your photographer has ever taken slides of you and if so would you please quote me your price.

Thanks very much for your, oh so personal autograph on my last picture and your very sweet note on your form letter.

Well Patti leaving for Northern California for about a month and hoping to hear from you upon my return Oct 1st.

Yours sincerly
Eugene H. Smith

A KIMBERLING ENTERPRISE

Coca-Cola
THE CRAY TAYLOR
HOTEL & APTS
Coca-Cola
THE CRAY TAYLOR
APARTMENT HOTEL
THE CRAY TAYLOR
HOTEL & APTS.
Coca-Cola

(I changed my address, I moved to my present address a couple of weeks ago which is on the envelope)

Indianapolis, Ind

Dec. 11, 1961

Dear Patti:

Hello "Miss Educated Torso." "I'm" hoping this letter finds you in the best of spirits ---Christmas that is!!

By the way I'm fan number 606 but I sure hope I was first but I'm sure you give all your fans the same loveable treatment, which is O.K. by me. Oh Yeah!

I want you to know Patti that the Photograph you sent me a few months ago is Delishous – er I mean Loveable.

I'm not ordering another one for the simple reason that I'm still carzy about the first one. But the second that watching your Photo makes me feel like – Ho Hum (Sleepy) I'll jump right up and order another. Okay by you?

I see you when you were here last winter and I havent' got over you yet. I've been looking forward to seeing you again this season but a big disappointment came up – for me and I'm sure the rest of your fans here. Mr. Clamage, the manager of our local Burlesque theatre (Fox) decided to eliminate stage shows (for the winter only I hope) and show art moves only. Chee!! Well anyway I'm sure we will all be hoping.

I was talking to Mr Clamage couple of days ago, and he said that Rene Andre commited suicide last January. She was also in Burlesque so I'm sure you must have known her. I saw her here about 8 years ago. But what I can't understand is this. Since offering merchandise presumabley through another firm there in Hollywood. Which I ordered and received and payed for by Postal Money Order. I also sent her greetings cards for both Valentine and Easter. Just a month ago I received an answer to a letter I sent her offering merchandise which I sent for and received with the money order

made payable in her name.

If his suicide was true the letters should have been returned to me. And I'm sure the money orders could not be cashed by another person. I'm sure you will be kind enough Patti to answer as soon as you find time and confirm this.

The way things stand now Im all mixed up so I'll be waiting for your answer to unmix me. Well it's about Santa Clause time so I'll be wishing you a Merry Christmas and a happy New Year to you.

The Best of Everything, nice, to you Patti. Thinking you, I remain your crazy fan. Carzy over you that is.

Thomas Costa

BURBANK
ON STAGE IN PERSON
PATTI WAGGIN
AND HER EDUCATED TORSO
GIRLS BEAUTIFUL ON THE STAGE GIRLS
ARMY
HOT DOGS
BURRITOS
TACOS

Patti on Wheels

Patti's love affair with motorcycles began while she was married to Doug Craig, who spent a great deal of time building and rebuilding bikes during World War II.

When Patti moved to Chico, she worked the burlesque circuit by night and the dirt bike circuit when the sun shone on the weekends. Instead of riding though, Patti was handing out the trophies and providing the winners with an obligatory kiss on the cheek to seal the victory. Of course, while in Chico Patti also claimed a victory of her own, capturing the heart of bike enthusiast and salesman Bill Brownell, at least for a while. No doubt this relationship only deepened Patti's love of powerful, fast cycles.

During her trip to Honolulu, friends caught Patti on film riding a bike of a different sort, a tricycle. That photo ended up in her personal scrapbook with the caption "getting a new bike."

When she wasn't riding a motorcycle, Patti's vehicle of choice was a fast ragtop convertible. There was not much opportunity for cycle riding during Patti's marriage to Don Rudolph however. Don himself could not ride as there was a clause in his contract against it. So, Patti transferred her need for speed to Kart Racing while Don was playing ball, introduced to the sport by Rudolph's brothers and nephews. Little more than powerful lawnmower engines attached to go karts, they were entertaining and went fast, and that was enough for Patti.

Patti made several attempts to get magazine writers to cover the sport, but they refused unless Patti was willing to provide some alluring poses alongside the karts. Given her love of her in- laws and the sport, Patti declined, repeatedly, despite the best efforts of persistent editors to change her mind. Patti's passion for speedy vehicles remained, but her days as Patti Waggin were drawing to a close. Her life as Patricia Rudolph was replacing it.

CLEANING

22
ARIEL

33
53

Your Order Now
FOR THE NEW
74

CALIFORNIA 40
44 81

Los Angeles, Calif.
July 1961

Miss Patti Waggin,

A few lines to wish you luck a plenty. Back from Las Vegas. Later on I will ask you for more of your photos. Had received all with all kindness tenderness.

I enclose & send you a small photo of you I came across.

Most Sincerely yours Friend-Fan Hoping to receive a nice letter from you so long.

Robert Hernandez
1619 E. Santa Barbara Ave.
Los Angeles 11, Calif.

I might move to Las Vegas soon. I will write you as ask you for a pin up photo.

Your Sincerely Robert
God Bless You
Bye

Author's Note: Patti wrote on the bottom of the letter in red pencil "Write & thank him for the photo of Betty Page when I send new address also Christmas Card."

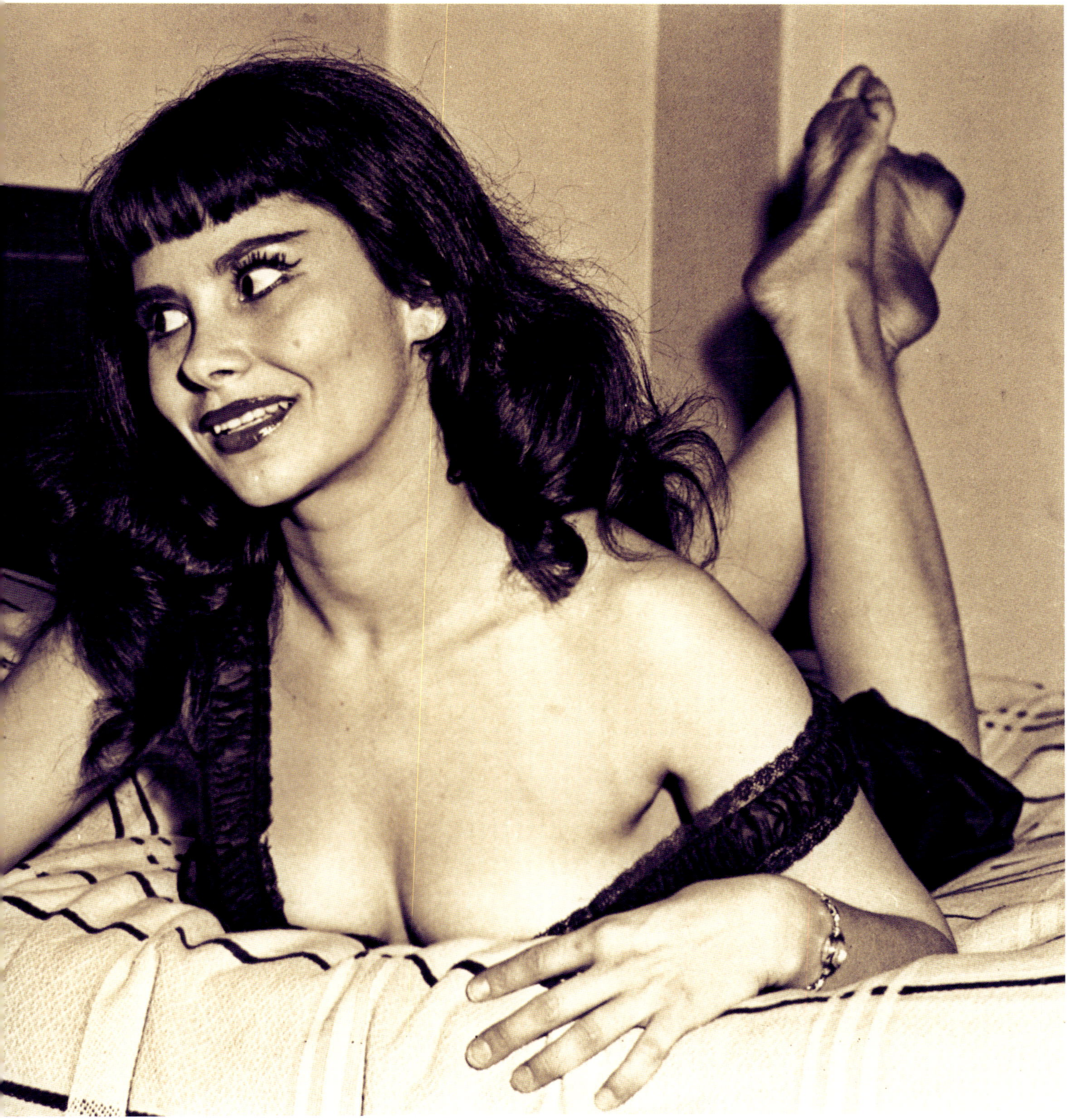

6/13/61

Hi Patti

I'm sure you and I will remain friends for a long time. I liked you last letter very much. Without real friends this would certainly be a dull world.

Incidently an outdoor Art show is given every year in the Village in N.Y. (Greenwich Village) and I always manage to pick up some nice work of art, etc. I got you some nice ear rings all hand made – with "gold fish" in a black casing. I think you'll like them. These are real gold fishes but of course small enough to be inserted in ear rings.

I will send them in a separate package. Hope you like them. If you don't you can give them to someone friend of yours OK?

Remember you'r so nice and I wish to remain your friend forever so seldom you meet a person like yourself.

Love Vincent

Down the Home Stretch

Life with Don Rudolph was simplicity itself. Patti worked on the stage for as long as she wanted to, quitting when she felt she was past her prime. She traveled with Don as often as Don could arrange it, exchanging the role of Patti Waggin burlesque queen for Patti Rudolph baseball wife. By thirty-five, Patti and Don had a home and their one and only child, Artanya Julena.

By the mid-1960s, Don was playing in the major leagues for Washington. The Senators were not terribly good but they had their moments. In 1963, Don was named as Opening Day pitcher and was present while President John F. Kennedy threw out the first ball, the last first ball Kennedy would ever toss.

Patti was there for Opening Day, watching the game and capturing the moment with her Brownie camera. She made bigger headlines than the Senators. The local paper reported sighting the former stripper behind the camera as the handsome president looked toward her husband who was to throw the first pitch. That was April 8, 1963, and the only blemish on an otherwise picture perfect day was that the Senators lost to Baltimore 3-1, despite a good effort on the mound by Don.

Don Rudolph remained with Washington until 1965, when the Senators wanted to return him to the minors. Declining offers in Hawaii and Buffalo, Don chose to retire himself, turning his attentions to his fledgling company, California Underground Utilities.

In 1968, when Julena was only seven years old, tragedy struck. Don was killed in a trucking accident not far from home. Patti's loving "Daddy Donnie," author of daily love letters to Patti when he was on the road for spring training, was suddenly gone. With him went the family's security as well.

It would take a while for Patti to regain her balance, as stated at the start of this journey. She lived for her daughter and was supported by friends. Life would never be the same again for Patti, but it was not all bad. On February 24, 1992, Patricia Artae (Patti Waggin) Rudolph passed away at the age of sixty-six.

Patti has now left the stage, but she's left us all with this tale of her passing, captured in the photos and the letters you have seen here.

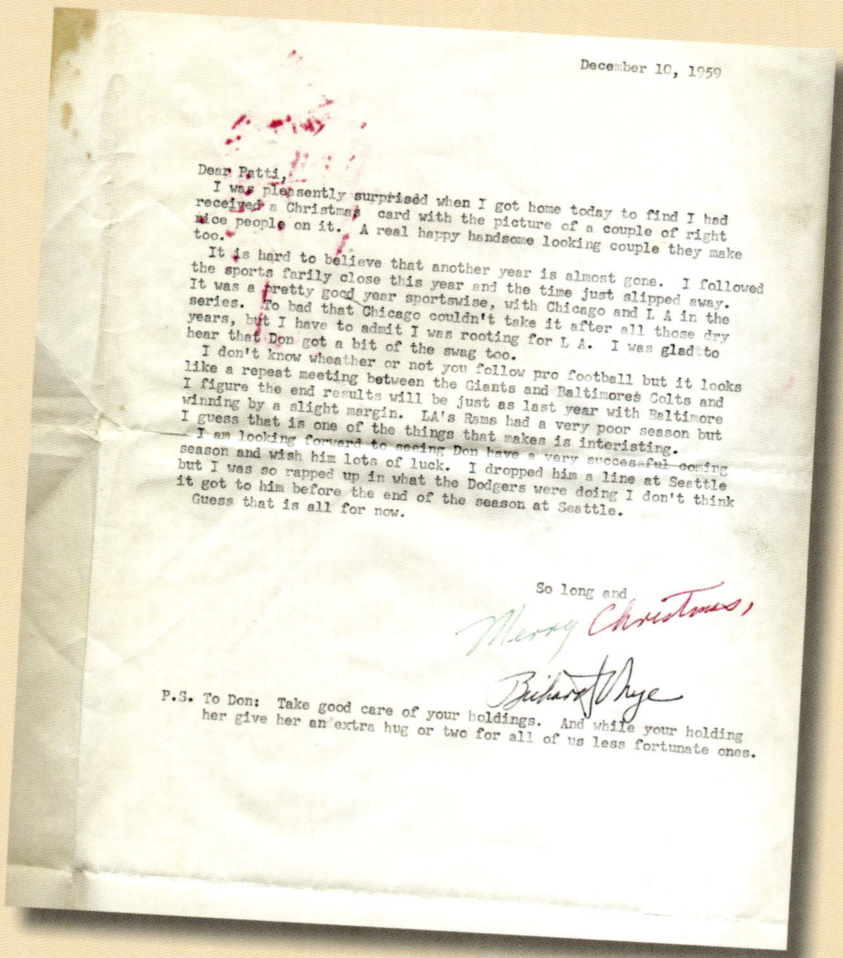

December 10, 1959

Dear Patti,
I was pleasently surprised when I got home today to find I had
received a Christmas card with the picture of a couple of right
nice people on it. A real happy handsome looking couple they make
too.
It is hard to believe that another year is almost gone. I followed
the sports farily close this year and the time just slipped away.
It was a pretty good year sportswise, with Chicago and L A in the
series. To bad that Chicago couldn't take it after all those dry
years, but I have to admit I was rooting for L A. I was glad to
hear that Don got a bit of the swag too.
I don't know wheather or not you follow pro football but it looks
like a repeat meeting between the Giants and Baltimores Colts and
I figure the end results will be just as last year with Baltimore
winning by a slight margin. LA's Rams had a very poor season but
I guess that is one of the things that makes is interisting.
I am looking forward to seeing Don have a very successful coming
season and wish him lots of luck. I dropped him a line at Seattle
but I was so rapped up in what the Dodgers were doing I don't think
it got to him before the end of the season at Seattle.
Guess that is all for now.

So long and
Merry Christmas,

P.S. To Don: Take good care of your holdings. And while your holding her give her an extra hug or two for all of us less fortunate ones.

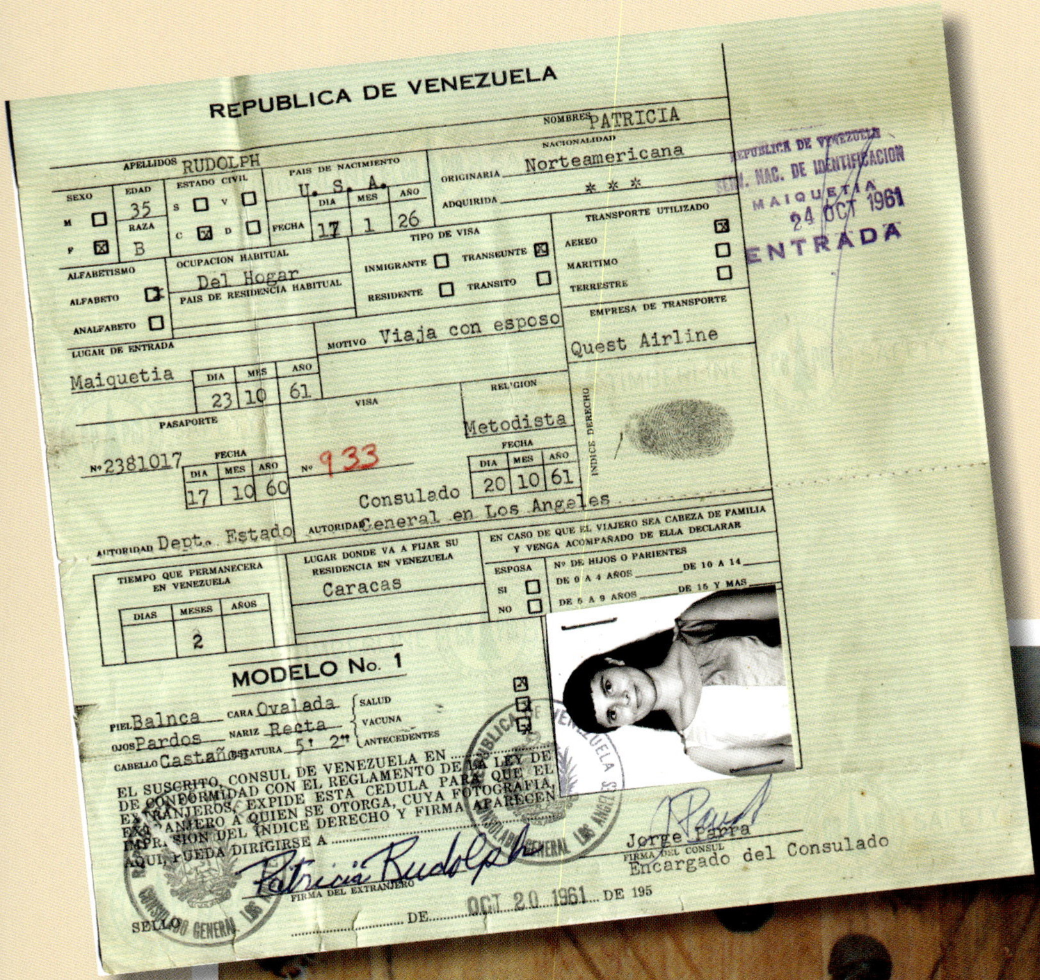

REPUBLICA DE VENEZUELA

NOMBRES PATRICIA

APELLIDOS RUDOLPH

NACIONALIDAD — ORIGINARIA Norteamericana — ADQUIRIDA * * *

SEXO: M ☐ F ☒ — EDAD 35 — RAZA B — ESTADO CIVIL: S ☐ V ☐ C ☒ D ☐

PAIS DE NACIMIENTO U. S. A. — FECHA: DIA 17, MES 1, AÑO 26

ALFABETISMO: ALFABETO ☒ ANALFABETO ☐

OCUPACION HABITUAL Del Hogar

PAIS DE RESIDENCIA HABITUAL

TIPO DE VISA: INMIGRANTE ☐ TRANSEUNTE ☒ RESIDENTE ☐ TRANSITO ☐

TRANSPORTE UTILIZADO: AEREO ☒ MARITIMO ☐ TERRESTRE ☐

EMPRESA DE TRANSPORTE Quest Airline

MOTIVO Viaja con esposo

LUGAR DE ENTRADA Maiquetia — DIA 23, MES 10, AÑO 61

RELIGION Metodista

PASAPORTE Nº 2381017 — FECHA: DIA 17, MES 10, AÑO 60 — AUTORIDAD Dept. Estado

VISA Nº 933 — FECHA: DIA 20, MES 10, AÑO 61 — AUTORIDAD Consulado General en Los Angeles

INDICE DERECHO

REPUBLICA DE VENEZUELA SERV. NAC. DE IDENTIFICACION MAIQUETIA 24 OCT 1961 ENTRADA

TIEMPO QUE PERMANECERA EN VENEZUELA: DIAS — MESES 2 — AÑOS

LUGAR DONDE VA A FIJAR SU RESIDENCIA EN VENEZUELA Caracas

EN CASO DE QUE EL VIAJERO SEA CABEZA DE FAMILIA Y VENGA ACOMPAÑADO DE ELLA DECLARAR: ESPOSA SI ☐ NO ☐ — Nº DE HIJOS O PARIENTES: DE 0 A 4 AÑOS ___ DE 5 A 9 AÑOS ___ DE 10 A 14 ___ DE 15 Y MAS ___

MODELO No. 1

PIEL Balnca — CARA Ovalada — SALUD ☒ VACUNA ☒ ANTECEDENTES ☒

OJOS Pardos — NARIZ Recta

CABELLO Castaños — ESTATURA 5' 2"

EL SUSCRITO, CONSUL DE VENEZUELA EN .... DE CONFORMIDAD CON EL REGLAMENTO DE LA LEY DE EXTRANJEROS, EXPIDE ESTA CEDULA PARA QUE EL EXTRANJERO A QUIEN SE OTORGA, CUYA FOTOGRAFIA, IMPRESION DEL INDICE DERECHO Y FIRMA APARECEN AQUI, PUEDA DIRIGIRSE A ....

Patricia Rudolph
FIRMA DEL EXTRANJERO

Jorge Parra
FIRMA DEL CONSUL
Encargado del Consulado

SELLO .... DE .... OCT 20 1961 ... DE 195

CONSULADO GENERAL LOS ANGELES — REPUBLICA DE VENEZUELA

With new daughter Artanya Julena Rudolph.

Most women would kill to look like this so soon after having a baby. Patti gave thanks for the fit body she developed over the years and kept.

So what do retired strippers do now they are off the stage? Spend time in their new kitchen, what else?

Many years past her stage days, Patti passed on what she knew to a younger generation.

My Darling Dearest Sweetheart,
P.S. We stay at the TEXAS STATE HOTEL HOUSTON, TEXAS
WHEW!
Boy! am I glad the season is over. Now it is just a matter of days before we are together or we get extra money.
but there certainly won't be any inspiration when I pitch. I love you and miss you so very much I can't stand it. All my love belongs to only you and without you I am lost and dead. I love you and love you with all my heart. All my undying love is for you forever & I'll never live without you.
I LOVE ONLY YOU.